Murder & Mayhem
in North London

TRUE CRIME FROM WHARNCLIFFE

Foul Deeds and Suspicious Deaths Series

Barking, Dagenham & Chadwell Heath
Barnet, Finchley and Hendon
Barnsley
Bath
Bedford
Birmingham
Black Country
Blackburn and Hyndburn
Bolton
Bradford
Brighton
Bristol
Cambridge
Carlisle
Chesterfield
Colchester
Cotswolds, The
Coventry
Croydon
Derby
Dublin
Durham
Ealing
Fens, In and Around
Folkstone and Dover
Grimsby
Guernsey
Guildford
Halifax
Hampstead, Holborn and St Pancras
Huddersfield
Hull
Jersey
Leeds
Leicester
Lewisham and Deptford
Liverpool
London's East End
London's West End
Manchester
Mansfield
More Foul Deeds Birmingham
More Foul Deeds Chesterfield
More Foul Deeds Wakefield
Newcastle
Newport
Norfolk
Northampton
Nottingham
Oxfordshire
Pontefract and Castleford
Portsmouth
Rotherham
Scunthorpe
Shrewsbury and Around Shropshire
Southampton
Southend-on-Sea
Staffordshire and The Potteries
Stratford and South Warwickshire
Tees
Uxbridge
Warwickshire
Wigan
York

OTHER TRUE CRIME BOOKS FROM WHARNCLIFFE

A-Z of London Murders, The
A-Z of Yorkshire Murders, The
Black Barnsley
Brighton Crime and Vice 1800-2000
Crafty Crooks and Conmen
Durham Executions
Essex Murders
Executions & Hangings in Newcastle
   and Morpeth
Great Hoaxers, Artful Fakers and
   Cheating Charlatans
Norfolk Mayhem and Murder
Norwich Murders
Plot to Kill Lloyd George
Romford Outrage
Strangeways Hanged
Unsolved Murders in Victorian &
   Edwardian London
Unsolved London Murders
Unsolved Norfolk Murders
Unsolved Yorkshire Murders
Warwickshire's Murderous Women
Yorkshire Hangmen
Yorkshire's Murderous Women

Please contact us via any of the methods below for more information or a catalogue
WHARNCLIFFE BOOKS
47 Church Street, Barnsley, South Yorkshire, S70 2AS
Tel: 01226 734555 • 734222 • Fax: 01226 734438
email: enquiries@pen-and-sword.co.uk
website: www.wharncliffebooks.co.uk

Murder & Mayhem in North London

GEOFFREY HOWSE

This book is dedicated to my good friend
BRENDAN E McNALLY

First Published in Great Britain in 2010 by
Wharncliffe Local History
an imprint of
Pen and Sword Books Ltd
47 Church Street
Barnsley
South Yorkshire
S70 2AS

Copyright © Geoffrey Howse 2010

ISBN: 978-184563-099-7

Typeset in Plantin by Concept, Huddersfield.

Printed and bound in England by
CPI Antony Rowe, Chippenham, Wiltshire.

Pen & Sword Books Ltd incorporates the Imprints of
Pen & Sword Aviation, Pen & Sword Maritime,
Pen & Sword Military, Wharncliffe Local History,
Pen & Sword Select, Pen & Sword Military Classics,
Leo Cooper, Remember When, Seaforth Publishing and
Frontline Publishing.

For a complete list of Pen & Sword titles please contact
PEN & SWORD BOOKS LIMITED
47 Church Street
Barnsley
South Yorkshire
S70 2BR
England
E-mail: enquiries@pen-and-sword.co.uk
Website: www.pen-and-sword.co.uk

Contents

Acknowledgements

ris Ackroyd, Michael Barber, Susan Barber, Susan Barnes, Joan Bostwick, Christine Boyce, Norma Braddick, Tracey Brown, Fred Calcott, Margaret Calcott, Sister S Choi, Robert A Dale, Kathleen Dale, Tobie Daniels, Chantelle Daniels, Thomas Roscoe Deane (1927–2009), Iris J Deller, Joanna C Murray Deller, Ricky S Deller, Tracy P Deller, Carol Gardner, Jean Gardner, Chris Gill, John Goldfinch, Leo Gonzales, Barbara Griffiths, Frederick Griffiths, Leroy Griffiths, Geraldine Healy, Ann Howse, Doreen Howse, Joy Howse, Kathleen Howse, Dr Hidayat Hussein, Michael Kemp, Celia Langton, Raymond Mellor Jones, Charles Keane, Eamon Keane, Sister Julia Keane, Hannah McNally, Jenny McNally, Grace L McHenry, Victoria McNally, Mick McCready, Patrick Newley (1955–2009), Nial O'Connor, Gerry O'Halloran, Sharon Owen, Dr Sadanandan Manidas (Mani) (1953–2009), Eleanor Nelder, Stanley Nelder, Anthony Richards, Aydan Sener, Ian Senior (of North Islington Nursery School), Annie Souter, Jackie Thomas, Josie Thomas, Karen Thomas, Breda Toh, Adam R Walker, Anna Walker, Christine Walker, Darren J Walker, David Walker, Emma C Walker, Ivan P Walker, Jenny Walker, Paula L Walker, Polly Walker, Thomas A Walker, Dave Webster, Terry Webster, Clifford Willoughby, Margaret Willoughby, the staff of the British Library, the staff of the British Library Newspaper Archive at Colindale, the staff of The National Archive at Kew, the staff of the Guildhall Library, Hornsey Historical Society, Bruce Castle Museum, AWDF and also thanks to John D Murray who has assisted me over many years.

Introduction

n this book I have attempted to give the reader an insight into a broad cross-section of crimes committed in the area we know generally as North London but which also includes north-east and north-west London. I have included a variety of murders, some of them internationally famous cases, others, not so well known, some even obscure, but all serve to illustrate the wide variety of methods that man will use to do away with his fellow man. The earliest case I have included was one of the most sensational of the seventeenth century. The most up-to-date case I have included shocked the sensibilities of the North London public as recent as 2005. In my efforts to bring these cases to the printed page I have delved through countless books, documents, newspapers and manuscripts, in an attempt to provide a clear and concise account. I apologise unreservedly for any errors or omissions.

CHAPTER 1

Murder & Mayhem North London Style 1678–1909

Murder of a Magistrate, Primrose Hill, 1678

Sir Edmund Berry Godfrey was the victim of a murder shrouded in mystery and often described as the greatest unsolved crime of the seventeenth century. His death was veiled by intrigue and deceit and it is marked by a false confession that resulted in the execution of three innocent men for a crime they neither committed nor played any part in. Born into an ancient Kentish family, on 23 December 1621, he was educated at Westminster School and Christ Church, Oxford. In 1640, he entered Gray's Inn, at the Inns of Court. He abandoned his legal career and became a woodmonger and coal merchant, and became considerably wealthy. By the late 1660s he was spending some of his time in politics and was becoming well known as a justice of the peace. As a result of the assistance he gave through his business enterprises during the plague, he was held in high regard. Similarly, his reaction following the Great Fire of London in 1666, during which he suffered personal injury while helping others, made him a notable figure at court, and he was rewarded for his services with a knighthood.

Sir Edmund Berry Godfrey.
Author's collection

Godfrey's death appears to have come about as a result of his involvement, in his capacity as a magistrate, in the swearing of documents concerning the conspiracy known to history as the 'Popish Plot'; which was later proven to be completely false and was in fact the invention of

Dr Titus Oates, clergyman, and Dr Israel Tonge, Presbyterian minister and scientist. Just as the details of the plot were being openly discussed, the killing of the highly regarded Protestant magistrate Sir Edmund Berry Godfrey caused panic on the streets of London.

Witnesses reported having last seen Godfrey on 12 October 1678. On the evening of Thursday 17 October, his body was found in a drainage ditch on Greenberry Hill (now known as Barrow Hill), one of the slopes at the southern edge of Primrose Hill. Sir Edmund was lying face down, impaled on a sword. The hilt was beneath the body and the blade pointed upwards. He had also been strangled and beaten about the body. In December 1678, Catholic silversmith, Miles Prance, then detained for conspiracy, confessed under torture to complicity in Godfrey's murder. His evidence was corroborated by the informer, William Bedloe. Three men were named in the plot – Robert Green, Henry Berry and Lawrence Hill. They were arrested and convicted on the flimsiest circumstantial evidence and hanged. Prance's confession was afterwards declared false and he pleaded guilty to perjury. Was it simply coincidence that the surnames of the three executed men spelled out the exact spot where Sir Edmund Berry Godfrey's body was found, Greenberry Hill?

Murder in Millfield Lane, Highgate, 1814

A violent murder took place on 4 October 1814, at Millfield Farm, a cottage situated in Millfield Lane, then a narrow thoroughfare, pretty much as it is today, which runs along part of the eastern edge of Hampstead Heath, adjacent to Highgate Ponds. The body of Elizabeth Buchanan (also known as Mrs Dobbins), a washer-woman, was found in the kitchen. She lived with her common-law husband, named Dobbins, who worked as a turncock for the Hampstead Water Company. Mrs Dobbins had been savagely beaten about the head with a poker, which had been left nearby covered with blood and bent with the force of the blows. At about the same time the body was discovered, a vagrant named Thomas Sharpe, had been apprehended as he retreated furtively towards Highgate Hill carrying two bundles of washing, stolen from Millfield Farm and he had been seen in the vicinity by several witnesses. The implausible story he told about buying the bundles from gypsies was not believed. At his trial, Lord Ellenborough,

Millfield Cottage, formerly Millfied Farm, Millfield Lane, Highgate, where Elizabeth Buchanan was murdered. The Author

having passed the death sentence, concluded with the words: '. . . and may the Lord have mercy on your soul'. Sharpe replied: 'May the curse of God attend you day and night, both in this world and the next.'

Johan Steinberg, multi-murderer and self-killer, Clerkenwell, 1834

John Steinberg, a German, was a forty-five-year-old whipmaker. He lived with Ellen Lefevre, aged twenty-five, a lady later described as his mistress, and their four children aged between six years and eight months, at 17 Southampton Street, now renamed Calshot Street, a turning off the Pentonville Road. On 8 September 1834 Steinberg murdered Ellen and their children by cutting all their throats from ear to ear. He then fell upon the knife, without leaving any explanation or clues as to his motives. Ellen and the children were buried by public subscription in the churchyard of the parish church of St James, Clerkenwell. Steinberg was buried in the Pauper's Burial Ground, Ray Street. In lieu of the old custom of driving a stake through the body, Steinberg's skull was broken with an iron mallet.

Policeman murdered, Hornsey Wood, 1842

In 1842, Hornsey Wood covered what is now the park itself, in the part of the capital known as Finsbury Park. A hostelry known as the *Hornsey Wood Tavern* once stood close to the site of the present-day boating pond. Near this pub, on 5 May 1842, Thomas Cooper, a twenty-two-year-old bricklayer-turned-thief, was surprised by a policeman, Charles Moss, while he was engaged in some felonious act. Without hesitation Cooper shot and wounded Moss. The sound of gunfire attracted the attention of another policeman called Mallet, and a baker called Mott, who was walking in the woods nearby.

Mallett and Mott gave chase as Cooper headed off in the direction of Highbury. Meanwhile, another baker, named Howard, was driving his post-chaise down Hornsey Road. He saw Cooper being chased and raced after him. Cooper headed for Highbury Barn. As another policeman, Timothy Daly, closed in on Cooper near Highbury Cottage, the latter jumped over a hedge into a short cul-de-sac called Black Ditch. This area was bounded by a paling fence which hemmed Cooper in long enough for Daly and Howard to catch up. Cooper, who was carrying two large horse pistols, fired both of them. One hit its target and Daly died instantly, but Hudson was unscathed and, with the help of two gardeners, was able to overcome Cooper and hold him. Cooper was tried at the Old Bailey, found guilty of murder and hanged outside Newgate on 4 July 1842.

Two Amorous Young Bucks, Primrose Hill, 1845

At around 7.00pm on 23 February 1845, Police Constable John Baldock, on patrol near the bridle path that ran through the fields between Primrose Hill and Belsize Park, was alerted by a baker, Edward Hilton, to cries of 'murder'. When he arrived at the scene (at today's junction of Belsize Park Gardens, England's Lane, Eton Avenue and Primrose Hill), accompanied by Sergeant Thomas Fletcher, in the dark they found the bloody and battered body of a well-dressed man. Whilst the sergeant went to get assistance, Constable Baldock stayed with the corpse.

A cloaked man, later identified as Thomas Hocker, approached the constable and uttered the words, 'Hallo, policeman, what have you got there.' He offered the constable brandy, which he refused, but Hocker persuaded him to take a shilling to get a glass of brandy later. At no time did he indicate that he knew the victim, although it would become clear that in fact he knew him very well. Shortly after William Satterthwaite, a Hampstead shoemaker, appeared, Hocker left the scene. Dr Perry examined the body. His report stated:

Thomas Hocker. Author's collection

> Death is attributed to concussion of the brain, the consequence of the external violence. I should image the wounds were inflicted by a heavy instrument, such as a stick ...

The man appeared to have been robbed, because the only item found on him was a letter written in blue ink addressed to J Cooper. The letter began: 'Dear James' and in it the writer requested a meeting at their usual place; she also informed him that she was pregnant. It was signed Caroline. A coroner's inquest was held at the *Yorkshire Grey* in Hampstead, by which time the victim had been identified as James De La Rue. A verdict of wilful murder was recorded. Twenty-seven-year-old James De La Rue, a music teacher, lived in well appointed lodgings, at 55 Whittlebury Street. The road no longer exists but in 1845 it led into Euston Square from Drummond Street, which straddles Hampstead Road. He earned his money principally giving piano lessons. James De La Rue was buried in St John's churchyard, Hampstead, on 28 February. Thomas Hocker, aged twenty-two, was a close friend of De La Rue. He lived at 11 Victoria Place, situated near the western edge of Regent's Park, sharing a room with his brother, James. Although he considered his musical talents to be worthy of more, he scraped a living by giving the occasional violin lesson.

These friends were a pair of amorous aspiring gentlemen, dapper dressers, who had a penchant for collecting pornography in the form of prints. Using various aliases, they had developed acquaintances with numerous women, mostly servant girls and those who, although not exactly prostitutes, had loose morals. They often indulged in orgies. Neither had any intention of cementing any of their relationships by marriage, hence the use of false names in their liaisons. During the police investigation that followed, De La Rue's friendship with Hocker emerged. Following the funeral, Hocker's apparent indifference to his best friend's death, threw suspicion his way. Both Thomas and James Hocker were questioned and, as matters unfolded, James Hocker was able to give information about the letter found in De La Rue's greatcoat pocket. The letter, written in a supposedly girlish hand, had in fact been written by Thomas Hocker in one of his numerous false hands. The unusual blue ink was traced to his room, and this evidence, together with the discovery of De La Rue's watch and a pair of blood-soaked trousers, proved sufficient to convict him of his friend's murder.

Hocker was tried at the Old Bailey, on 11 April, before Mr Justice Coleman, in a trial lasting less than ten hours. The jury found him guilty after just ten minutes deliberation. He protested his innocence to the end, blaming a person he would not name. He was hanged at Newgate, before a crowd of 10,000, on 28 April 1845, by William Calcraft.

Dreadful Tragedy at Lower Edmonton, 1866

On Boxing Day, Wednesday 26 December 1866, a dreadful tragedy took place at Lower Edmonton. For some years, a coachman, William Gudgeon and his wife Ann, a hard-working woman, had occupied a six-roomed house opposite the Great Eastern Railway Station. They had five children, the eldest of them aged fourteen. On Christmas Day 1866, Ann Gudgeon had complained to her husband that she was feeling unwell and she went to bed at 7.00pm. That night, at eleven o'clock, she got up and went downstairs and joined her husband and children. They remained up for an hour and then the whole family retired to bed. Mr and Mrs Gudgeon slept in a bed in the top front room of the house and in a corner of the same room was a bed made up for three of the children. As Ann Gudgeon was going to bed she looked very wild, and she said to her husband:

The light of the candle stares in my eyes. Put it out.

William Gudgeon did as his wife requested and then fell asleep. At that time the Gudgeons' youngest child, a six-month-old baby girl named Elizabeth, was lying fast asleep in her father's bed.

At two o'clock on Boxing Day morning, ten-year-old Selina Gudgeon was woken by some warm liquid being spattered over her face. When she opened her eyes she was confronted by her mother kneeling upon the dead body of her little brother, Timothy George, who had been lying asleep alongside of his sister Sarah Ann. Little Timothy's throat had been cut in the most fearful manner and blood was gushing from the wound. Ann Gudgeon looked very excited and she was brandishing an open razor, covered with blood, in her left hand. When she saw she had woken Selina she leaned over towards her daughter and caught hold of her. Selina screamed, then a fearful struggle ensued. In an attempt to protect herself Selina caught hold of the bedclothes and held them to her throat. She cried out:

> Oh mother why do you not put the razor down? You have killed Timothy and now you want to murder us.

Selina managed to wriggle out of bed and ran to the doorway, and rushed down the stairs followed by her mother, who continued to hold the open razor in her hand. On reaching the bottom of the stairs the girl ran into the lower front room. Her mother rushed past her and ran to the fireplace. Selina felt around in the dark until she felt a matchbox which was lying on the table. She struck a light and was horrified to see her mother in the dim light the match produced, cutting her throat. Blood gushed from the wound Ann Gudgeon had inflicted on herself and, as the match went out in the darkness, Selina Gudgeon heard her mother fall to the ground.

Selina ran upstairs and into her father's room, which was much lighter as light flooded in through the window from a street lamp outside. William Gudgeon was in a sound sleep and by his side lay the dead body of the baby, with her throat cut from ear to ear. Selina woke her father and told him what had occurred. William Gudgeon quickly dressed and ran out of the house to fetch a neighbour, Mrs Robinson, the wife of a railway employee. Meanwhile, Selina went to another room and woke her brother, Thomas and sent him off to the police station. Police Sergeant Howlett accompanied the boy back to the scene of the tragedy. When Sergeant Howlett entered the parlour he found the dead body of Ann Gudgeon lying near the fireplace. Her head rested on the fender and there was an open, black-handled razor, lying on her breast.

Dr O'Brien, of Church Street, Edmonton was called to the scene. He said the woman's wound was self-inflicted and must

Ann Gudgeon, having cut her little son's throat, turns her attention to her daughter.
Illustrated Police News

have caused almost instantaneous death. The police and the doctor then went upstairs to examine the bodies of the two children. Timothy Gudgeon was lying in a pool of blood. Dr O'Brien expressed the opinion that death must have been instantaneous. The baby had been killed in a similar manner.

On Saturday 29 December, the coroner for the Duchy of Lancaster, Mr J W Payne, opened the inquiry at the *Cross Keys Inn*, Lower Edmonton, in connection to the murder of Timothy Gudgeon and Elizabeth Gudgeon by their mother, Ann Gudgeon, who afterwards committed suicide. After hearing the evidence the jury returned a verdict that Timothy Gudgeon and Elizabeth Gudgeon had been wilfully murdered by Ann Gudgeon, and that

Ann Gudgeon committed suicide by cutting her throat while in a state of unsound mind.

Eleanor Pearcey, Kentish Town, 1890

Mrs Pearcey, as this particular murderess preferred to be known, was in fact not married, nor was her surname Pearcey. Her real name was Mary Eleanor Wheeler, but after she went to live with a man named Pearcey in Camden Town, at the age of sixteen, she assumed his name and the title of his wife. Pearcey left her but she retained his surname until the day she died. By the beginning of 1890, twenty-four-year-old Eleanor Pearcey was emotionally unstable, depressed and lonely. She had few relatives, just an elderly mother and an older sister. She was a kept woman, her ground floor apartment consisting of three rooms in a house at 2 Priory Street (now Ivor Street), situated on the border of Kentish Town with Camden Town, being paid for by her admirer, Charles Chrichton, of Gravesend, in Kent, who visited her once a week. Another admirer, a furniture remover called Frank Hogg, she was particularly fond of and would place a light in her window to let him know when she was free. Hogg was not as emotionally attached to Mrs Pearcey as she was to him. He used to see other women. One of them, a thirty-one-year-old spinster named Phoebe, who was known to Eleanor Pearcey, became pregnant. This hapless lothario was virtually forced into marriage by Phoebe's family and in due course Phoebe Hogg was delivered of a baby girl, also called Phoebe.

The marriage was not a happy one and Frank used to pour out his woes to Eleanor Pearcey, who became jealous of his wife, which developed into deep hatred. The Hoggs lived in rooms, at 141 Prince of Wales Road, Kentish Town. On Thursday 23 October, Mrs Hogg received a note from Mrs Pearcey inviting her to tea, an invitation that was declined due to prior commitments. When another note arrived the next day Mrs Hogg accepted. She left her home at about 3.30pm, pushing little Phoebe in her bassinet. Mrs Pearcey's neighbours heard 'banging and hammering', some said they heard screams, coming from the Pearcey household at about 4.00pm. Phoebe Hogg had been killed in Mrs Pearcey's kitchen with a poker and more than one knife. She had clearly put up a struggle as both her arms were bruised and, as was later discovered, so were Mrs Pearcey's. Mrs Hogg's throat had been so savagely cut that her neck had been all but severed. That evening Mrs Pearcey put Mrs Hogg's body into the bassinet on top of the baby and covered it was an antimacassar. Little Phoebe had either already been suffocated or was smothered by the weight of her mother's body. Mrs Pearcey pushed the bassinet for six miles. Her first port of call was Crossfield Road near Swiss Cottage. There she unloaded Mrs Hogg, leaving her body in a partly-built house. She took a long walk up the Finchley Road to Cock and Hoop Field, where she dumped the baby's body and continued to push the empty bassinet until it collapsed outside 34 Hamilton Terrace, near Maida Vale, where she left it.

The bodies were discovered over the following two days. It was not long before the finger of suspicion was wagging at Mrs Pearcey. When the police visited her at Priory Street she ascribed the bloodstains in the kitchen to killing mice and calmly sat at the piano humming a tune. Eleanor Pearcey was charged with the murders of Mrs Phoebe Hogg and her baby. She was tried at the Old Bailey on 1 December. The trial lasted for four days. Found guilty, she was resentful that Frank Hogg had offered her no support. She couldn't grasp that in killing his baby daughter, his feelings for her had changed. She was hanged at Newgate on 23 December 1890, by executioner James Berry. As she was being led to the scaffold, Mrs Pearcey said to the chaplain, Mr Duffield: 'The sentence is just, but the evidence was false.'

The Masset Woman, Dalston Junction, 1899

There have been murders, particularly those perpetrated at the hands of a woman, where the feminine attributes of the so-called gentle sex, have worked favourably for the accused in a court of law, sometimes despite their obvious guilt, resulting in their acquittal. However, there are some crimes considered to be so abhorrent that, irrespective of the obvious attractions of the female concerned, the public can find not a grain of sympathy for the accused. One such murderess was Louise (or Louisa) Josephine Masset.

By 1899, when this murder occurred, Stoke Newington, an attractive and once isolated village had become another casualty in the rapidly growing expansion of suburban London. In-filled housing and early, mid and late Victorian villas covered its former agricultural land, even replacing some of the ancient buildings that once graced its streets. Thirty-six-year-old Louise Masset, the daughter of a French man and an English woman, lived in one such villa, at 29 Bethune Road. She was an attractive woman of genteel disposition, who earned her living as either a governess or piano teacher. She was unmarried and boarded at her sister's house.

An affair she had had in France had resulted in a child, a boy named Manfred Louis, who was in 1899 aged four. The boy's father's name was never divulged. Louise lodged Manfred with a foster-mother, Miss Helen Gentle, who lived in Clyde Road, Tottenham. Miss Gentle had looked after Manfred from being a few weeks old and Louise used to pay her for her son's upkeep; and she would take Manfred home to Stoke Newington, as and when her whims dictated. In Stoke Newington, Louise began having an affair with a French student, nineteen-year-old, Eudore Lucas. As the affair turned into a more meaningful relationship Louise came to realise that little Manfred was becoming an encumbrance. Her love life was being affected by his presence, Eudore's enthusiasm was waning and if she was to retain his affections, Manfred could no longer be part of her life. Louise decided on a plan of action and was quick to bring it to fruition.

Louise told Miss Gentle that Manfred's father was going to take over his upbringing in France and arranged to collect both him and his clothes, which had been placed in a parcel, on the morning of 27 October. The last reported sighting of Louise Masset and her son was at London Bridge station, at midday, where witnesses described the little boy as showing signs of distress. Later that same day, at 6.30pm, a dreadful discovery was made in the ladies' lavatory on Platform 3 at Dalston Junction station. Manfred's battered and naked body was found wrapped in a black shawl. A bloodstained stone lay nearby. The boy had been hit with the stone and strangled.

When reports of the dead child appeared in the newspapers, Miss Gentle, suspecting the worst, reported her suspicions to police. Having been taken to see the child's body, she was able to identify him as her former charge Manfred Masset. Under questioning, Louise said she had handed the boy over to two ladies on London Bridge. The ladies, she added, were starting an orphanage in Chelsea. She said she had given them £12 for her son's upkeep. She had then caught a train to Brighton where she had spent the weekend in company with her lover. However, Louise had not thought her plan through and had failed to adequately cover her tracks. Firstly, she said she had a receipt for the £12, supposedly handed over to the Chelsea baby-farmers (see below) but she failed to produce it, as it clearly didn't exist. Crucially, more damning evidence existed against her and it was soon to bring about her downfall. Foolishly, Louise had left the paper parcel containing Manfred's clothes in the waiting room at Brighton station. The link with the parcel and her known movements was soon established. The black shawl in which the little boy's body had been wrapped was identified as having been bought by Louise Masset in a shop in Stoke Newington. The final piece of incriminating evidence was the bloodstained stone. It fitted an indentation in the rockery at 29 Bethune Road exactly.

There was no outcry when this uncaring mother was found guilty of murder at the Old Bailey and sent to the gallows. The fact that she had killed her son, then callously gone off to Brighton with her lover, appalled the sensibilities of the general public. Before her execution she confessed she had killed Manfred to spare him the abuse that all too often confronts the illegitimate. The vanity of this woman seemed to know no bounds. Her confession failed to convince, as most people believed she had killed her son in her vain ambition to captivate and retain her young lover. Louise Masset has the dubious distinction of being the first person to be hanged in Great Britain in the twentieth century. She was hanged at Newgate, by James Billington, on 9 January 1900.

The Islington Baby-farming Case, 1903–4

Baby-farming was a peculiarity of late Victorian England: unwanted babies and children, whether illegitimate or simply a burden to their parents, were farmed out to women who acted as foster-mothers. These women were paid to 'adopt' the children or to look after them for a specific period, before they were moved to permanent homes. Large financial rewards could be obtained by taking these unwanted children and the result was that some women obtained money to place a child in a good home and, having found none, 'took care' of their charges simply by killing them. Rivers, canals, reservoirs and even rubbish tips were common dumping grounds for these unfortunate innocents. Two such baby-farmers were Amelia Sach and Annie Walters.

Mrs Amelia Sach, aged twenty-six, lived at Claymore House, Hertford Road, East Finchley, which she had converted to serve as a private lying-in hospital. There she operated a successful business as an *accoucheuse*. She claimed to be a certified midwife and nurse and attended to her female patients herself. In difficult cases she arranged for a doctor to be present. She had a ready supply of unwanted babies to baby-farm. Her accomplice in crime was fifty-one-year-old Annie Walters, who described herself as a 'short stay foster parent'. Exactly how many babies were killed by these evil women will never be known. Annie Walters often changed address, probably so her activities were not subjected to too close a scrutiny. While lodging at 11 Danbury Street, Islington, with a police constable named Sale and his wife, her many accounts of how babies were given new homes made him suspicious. Her fanciful stories did not ring true with PC Sale. He and a colleague, Detective Constable Wright, decided to watch her. On 18 November 1902, Annie Walters had in her possession a baby boy, believed to be the child of Ada Galley, a single young woman and a patient at Claymore House. Walters was followed to South Kensington railway station by DC Wright, who arrested her after the child was found to be dead. It had been dead for between eight and twelve hours. Chlorodyne, a painkiller containing morphia, chloroform and prussic acid, mixed with a baby's milk in sufficient quantity would soon cause death. Walters said to the police: 'I never murdered the dear. I only gave it two drops in its bottle, the same as I take myself.' A whole catalogue of grim events unfolded and Amelia Sach was also arrested. Both were charged with murder. Their trial commenced before Mr Justice Darling at the Old Bailey on 15 January 1903. Found guilty of murder they were sentenced to death. Mrs Sach's plea for clemency on the grounds that it was most unusual to be hanged as an accessory was turned down and the two women were executed together at Holloway Prison, by the Billington brothers, on 3 February 1903. Amelia Sach and Annie Walters were the first of only five women to be executed at Holloway (no men were executed there).

A Smell Under the Stairs and the Capture of a Bigamous Murderer, Queens Park, 1904

In 1904, William Dell rented part of a house from George Crossman in Ladysmith Avenue (later renamed Wrentham Avenue),

Queens Park. He complained to Mr Crossman about the appalling smell that was coming from a cupboard under the stairs. Crossman attributed the smell to a box of 'size' (a gelatinous substance used to prepare plaster for decoration, amongst other things) that had 'gone bad'. He assured his tenant he would have it removed. The box was in fact a tin trunk. Mr Dell was not convinced by Crossman's explanation and thought there might be something sinister occurring. He reported the matter to the police and, coincidentally, a constable called to investigate just as the trunk was being carried out by some workmen, while Crossman puffed on a cigar to mask the stench. When he saw the policeman, Crossman panicked and ran off, leaving behind a bemused constable and Mr Dell. They followed him, but as they closed in, he took a razor out of his pocket and cut his throat, dying where he fell. The trunk was opened and found to contain the remains of Ellen Sampson, encased in cement, which had cracked and released noxious smelling gasses. Crossman had bigamously married her more than a year previously, she being the fifth of seven women to have become his wife.

The Camden Town Murder, 1907

The Camden Town Murder is considered to be one of the most sensational unsolved murders of the twentieth century. Railway chef Bertram Shaw's job took him to Sheffield each evening and he returned to London the following morning. On the morning of 12 September 1907, he came home from work as usual to his lodgings at 29 St Paul's Road (now Agar Grove), Camden Town. He discovered that his sitting-room had been ransacked and when he forced open the locked bedroom door he found the naked body of his common-law wife, twenty-three-year-old Phyllis Dimmock, with her throat savagely cut.

Like Bertram, Phyllis worked the night-shift. She was a prostitute and was well known throughout the area. The *Rising Sun* in Euston Road was a well-known haunt of hers, as was *The Eagle* in Camden Town. A letter and a postcard found in her rooms and written in the same hand led police to a young man who had been seen with her at both public houses. Robert Wood was a talented artist who worked as an engraver at a glassmaker's, in Grays Inn Road, and also earned money as a freelance cartoonist. He lived in a comfortable home in St Pancras with his father. He was arrested on circumstantial evidence and charged with murder. The trial began at the Old Bailey on 12 December. Wood was defended by the brilliant Edward Marshall Hall. This case is significant for Wood being the first person accused of murder to be acquitted after giving evidence at his own trial (until the Criminal Evidence Act of 1898, the accused had previously not been allowed to give evidence in the witness box). Wood com-pletely charmed the jury, stuck to his original story concerning his

Phyllis Dimmock. Author's collection

version of events as told to the police and they acquitted him. Nobody else was ever implicated in this murder.

The Tottenham Outrage, 1909

On Saturday 23 January 1908, an extraordinary chase took place through North and North-East London. The murders associated with it became known as the 'Tottenham Outrage' and the chase came about after a pair of Latvian anarchists snatched the wages (£80, the equivalent of over £4,000 today) as they were delivered to Schnurrmann's rubber factory in Chesnut Road. Having grabbed the money, Paul Hefeld and Jacob Lepidus ran down Chesnut Road with a policeman chasing after them. They turned into Scales Road, then left into Dawlish Road and right into Mitchley Road. It was there, beside the Mission Hall, that Hefeld shot PC Tyler. Ten-year-old Ralph Jocelyn was also shot and killed as he ran for cover. Both victims were later buried in Abney Park Cemetery in Stoke Newington.

The chase continued along Park View Road, then over the rail-way into the marshes. The two men ran northwards until they reached Lockwood Reservoir, then, realising police reinforce-ments were waiting for them, they went east across Walthamstow Avenue to Chingford Road. There they hijacked a tram travelling south, still firing guns at their pursuers. The two men forced the conductor to show them how to operate the tram, the driver having fled, along with most of the passengers. The police requisitioned a milk cart in an attempt to follow the tram, but the anarchists shot the pony. They continued to fire their guns and in all over 400 rounds were fired. Fortunately, although seventeen civilians and seven policeman were injured, no one else was killed.

The two men then made their way through the railway arch that runs across the Ching Brook, where they found themselves confronted by a 6-foot fence that formed the boundary of a newly-built housing estate. Realising they were cornered, Hefeld panicked and shot himself in the head (dying of his injuries on 18 February), but Lepidus escaped over the fence, crossed the railway lines and made his way from Beech Hall Road towards fields bordering Prestons Avenue. A public house called the *Royal Oak* stood at the top of the avenue. He crossed Hale End Road to the rear of the pub and followed a hedge bordering some cottages. He lept over this hedge and entered Oak Cottage, the home of coal-carrier Charles Rolstone and his family. Then he ran upstairs and locked himself in the front bedroom. Several shots were exchanged but as the police closed in on him, Lepidus shot himself dead.

CHAPTER 2

The Case of the Müller Cut-down

Hackney Wick, 1864

... injuries to his head were consistent with the victim having been struck with a blunt instrument four or five times.

This case is remarkable for two principal reasons. Not only was this Britain's first railway murder, but also because the murderer, Franz Müller's name lived on, not simply as a notorious murderer but in the style of a hat.

On Saturday 9 July 1864, Mr Thomas Briggs, chief clerk in the bank of Messrs Robarts & Co, of Lombard Street, left the bank in the afternoon as was his usual custom. During the evening he dined with his niece and her husband, Mr and Mrs David Buchan, at 23 Nelson Square, Peckham (today's Furley Road), before he returned to the city to catch a suburban train on the North London Railway, which left Fenchurch Street station for Chalk Farm at 9.50pm. He travelled in a first-class carriage, No 69. Mr Briggs lived at 5 Clapton Square, near to the Hackney or Hackney Wick (Victoria Park) stations, in north-east London.

The train left the next station, Bow, at 10.01pm, Hackney Wick at 10.05pm and arrived at Hackney at approximately 10.11pm. At this station two bank clerks who were also employed by Messrs Robarts & Co, Henry Vernez and Sydney Jones, who had purchased tickets for Highbury, opened the door of a first-class compartment, which was unoccupied, got in and sat down. Almost immediately, Sydney Jones felt something wet and drew his companion's attention to some blood on his hand. They immediately left the carriage and summoned the guard of the train, Benjamin Ames. Mr Ames examined the compartment and discovered bloodstains on the cushions of the seat that backed onto the engine on the left-hand side of the train as it was going from Farringdon Station. There was blood on the glass by the cushion, some blood on the cushion opposite and on the offside handle of the carriage door. In the carriage the guard found a hat, a walking stick and a small black leather bag. He took these away and the carriage was locked. The train continued its journey to Chalk Farm and was later taken back to Bow. Mr Greenwood, the stationmaster at Chalk Farm, took charge of the hat, walking stick and bag, as lost property.

The driver and guard of a train, travelling through north-east London at about the same time as the hat, walking stick and bag were being handed to Mr Greenwood at Chalk Farm made an alarming discovery. They were taking a train of empty carriages from Hackney Wick Station to Fenchurch Street and had just crossed the railway bridge by Victoria Park, when William Timms, the guard, was alerted by Alfred Ekin, the engine driver, to something lying in the 6-foot way, between the Up and Down lines. They stopped the train and backed it up to where the object was lying. When they went to investigate they discovered the body of a man lying on his back with his head towards Hackney. Help was summoned from the nearby *Mitford Castle* public house and the body was carried along a path down the embankment at the side of the railway bridge and into the inn.

Police Constable K71, Edward Dougan, was quickly on the scene. Having detected sign of life he immediately sent for a surgeon, Vincent Merton Cooper. Before medical help arrived Police Constable Dougan searched the victim's pockets. In the left-hand trouser pocket he found four sovereigns and some keys; in the vest pocket a florin and half of a first-class railway ticket; in the right-hand trouser pocket 10s 6d in silver and copper, some more keys, a silver snuffbox, various letters and papers and a silk handkerchief. The man also wore a diamond ring on the little finger of his right hand and there was a gold fastening to his waistcoat. His identity was established by a bundle of letters in his pocket, which bore his full address:

T. Briggs, Esq.,
Robarts & Co.,
Lombard Street.

Mr Briggs had several severe wounds, apparently inflicted by a blunt instrument used to ferocious effect, and other injuries, bruises and contusions, which those who attended him following the attack suggested might have been sustained when he fell from the carriage. Mr Brigg's own surgeon, Francis Toulmin, of Lower Clapton, arrived at the *Mitford Castle* a little before 3.00am. He found Mr Briggs groaning but unconscious. He died at 11.45pm on Sunday night, approximately twenty-seven hours after the attack had taken place.

A post-mortem examination was carried out on the body of Thomas Briggs, on Tuesday 12 July, by Mr Francis Toulmin, attended by Mr Brereton, Mr Cooper and others. He descried the condition of Mr Briggs, who stood about 5 feet 9 inches tall and weighed between 11 and 12 stones:

> The cartilage of the left ear was severed by a jagged wound; about an inch anterior to the left ear ear was a deep wound, extending to the bone, if not into it. Over the temporal muscle was a contused wound – a superficial and grazed wound, not a deep wound. There were several incised wounds on the scalp, as many as four, and one other, near the crown of the head, behind the others 3 inches long, behind the vertex. It was an incised wound. The other wounds were about ¾ inch in length, having a direction all from behind to behind. That applies to all wounds on the top of the head. Those wounds all extended to the pericranium, but had not divided it. On removing the scalp the shell was found to be extremely fractured, the fissures extended in various directions, radiating from the centre. A portion of the outer commencement of the parietal bone, ¾ inch long and ½ inch wide, was perfectly separated, and fell out. There was an effusion of blood between the neck and the skull cap or calvarium. There was also a further effusion of blood between the skull cap and dura matter. The temporal bone was driven in upon the brain.

Mr Toulmin concluded that the superficial injuries sustained by Mr Briggs to the left side of his head were consistent with his fall from the railway carriage and the other injuries to his head were consistent with the victim having been struck with a blunt instrument four or five times.

The friends of Mr Briggs were communicated with, and it was ascertained that when he left home, the morning of the murderous attack, he wore gold-rimmed eye-glasses and a gold watch and chain. The stick and bag were his, but not the hat. A desperate struggle must have taken place in the carriage, and the stains of a bloody hand marked the door. The facts of the murder and its object, robbery, were thus conclusively proved. It was also easily established that the hat found in the carriage had been bought at Walker's hatters in Crawford Street, Marylebone, while, within a few days, Mr Brigg's gold chain was traced to a jeweller's, at 55 Cheapside. The jeweller, the aptly named Mr Death, had given another chain in exchange for it to a man thought to be a foreigner. More precise clues to the murderer's identity were not long wanting; indeed, the readiness with which they were produced and followed up, showed how the wide dissemination of news regarding a murder facilitates the detection of crime. In a little more than a week a cabman came forward and voluntarily made a statement which at once drew suspicion to a German, Franz Müller, who had been the man's lodger. Müller had given the cabman's little daughter a jeweller's cardboard box bearing the name of Mr Death. A photograph of Müller shown to the jeweller was identified as the likeness of the man who had exchanged Mr Brigg's chain. Last of all, the cabman swore that he had bought the very hat found in the carriage for Müller at Walker's of Crawford Street, Marylebone.

This fixed the crime squarely on Müller, who had already left the country, thus increasing the suspicion under which he lay. There was no mystery about his departure: he had gone to Canada by the *Victoria* sailing ship, starting from London docks and bound for New York. When these facts were established, two detectives armed with an arrest warrant, and accompanied by the jeweller and the cabman, went to Liverpool and took the first steamer across the Atlantic. This was the *City of Manchester*, and it was expected to arrive some days before the *Victoria*. When the sailing ship docked, the officers boarded the *Victoria* at once. Müller was identified by Mr Death, and the arrest was made. Mr Brigg's watch was found wrapped up in a piece of leather in the suspect's luggage, and at the time of his capture Müller was actually wearing Mr Brigg's hat, cut down and somewhat altered. The prisoner was extradited to England immediately. He and his escort arrived on 17 September.

Twenty-five-year-old Franz Müller, a native of Saxe-Weimar, had been apprenticed as a gunsmith in his native country and had arrived in England in 1862 hoping to find work. Unable to secure a job in his chosen trade, he found work as a tailor and was last employed in that capacity for a six-week period, up to 2 July 1864,

Left: Franz Müller. Right: Thomas Briggs, the victim of Britain's first railway murder. Author's collection

by Mr Hodgkinson, of Threadneedle Street, at 25 shillings a week. At the time of the murder Müller was lodging at 16 Park Terrace, which was part of the Old Ford Road, Victoria Park, Hackney.

His trial followed at the next sessions of the Central Criminal Court and began on 27 October 1864, before the Lord Chief Baron (Sir Frederick Pollock). It lasted for three days and ended in his conviction. The case was one of circumstantial evidence, but, as Sir Robert Collyer, the Solicitor General, pointed out, it was the strongest circumstantial evidence ever been brought forward in a murder case and it could not be explained away. Collyer cited the prisoner's poverty, his inability to account for himself on the night of the murder, and his possession of the property of the murdered man. An alibi was set up for the defence but not well substantiated, and without hesitation the jury returned a verdict of guilty.

Müller protested after sentence of death had been passed upon him that he had been convicted on a false statement of facts. He adhered to this almost to the very last. His case had been warmly espoused by the Society for the Protection of Germans in the United Kingdom, and powerful influence was exerted, both in

England and abroad, to obtain a reprieve. Müller knew that any confession would ruin his chances of escaping the gallows. His arguments were specious and evasive when pressed to confess:

> Why should man confess to man? Man cannot forgive man, only God can do so. Man is therefore only accountable to God.

Müller's execution took place on Tuesday 14 November 1864, outside Newgate Gaol. The executioner was William Calcraft. Below is part of an account by Frederick Wicks, a sub-editor of the *Globe*, who was actually present on the scaffold at Müller's execution:

> Dr Cappel, the minister stood close to Müller, with his feet on the very edge of the drop. I stood just behind him, but nearer the outside of the scaffold. The conversation was hurried. On Dr Cappel's part it earnest and excited, but Müller preserved the same stolid, unimpassioned manner that had characterised his attitude throughout. Calcraft, I noticed disappeared as soon as they began to speak, and I can see Dr Cappel now leaning forward, with both hands extended, as if to draw Müller's words to him as the drop fell and Müller disappeared. Calcraft had done his work well. One strong convulsion and all was over. But Dr Cappel didn't stay to see this. As soon as he recovered from the surprise and alarm caused by the unexpected fall of the drop he dashed down the stairs with his hands aloft, and shouted as he ran, 'Confessed, confessed, thank God!' After one more look at the crowd, now a roaring tumult swaying to and fro, I followed close at his heels and the whole company pressed round him in the chaplain's room, where he told the story of Müller's last words. Just before Müller dropped to his death, he called out 'Ich habe es getan' (I did it).

It is also worth noting part of the account of the execution from *The Times*, of 15 November 1864, which gives a further fascinating insight into the contemporary style of reporting a public execution:

> The time has been, and very lately too, when the dress in which a felon died, or even a cast of his distorted features, would have been worth their weight in gold. But nothing for this catering for the wretched curiosity of the gallows is permitted now. In whatever clothes or worse felons die, these whether good or bad are burnt before their burial, so that all that may be called the traces

of their crime are destroyed with its perpetrator ... there is no tomb but Newgate – a tomb such as the few who love the felon best can only leave with shuddering hope that it may be forgotten. In Newgate there is no solemnity of burial; it is a mere hurried covering of the body of one who was not fit to live among mankind. So with the corpse of Müller. It had died publicly; the surgeon had certified to its shameful death. Towards the middle of the day the rough deal box which held it was filled with shavings and quicklime, and the warders carried it out to the hole where it had to be thrust under the flagtones of a narrow, bleak gaol pathway. There, below the massive cross-barred gratings which almost shut out the light of day – there, where none pass the little hidden grave save those who, like himself, must go over it to their great tomb, the body of Müller rests. In a few days the cruelty and singularity of his great crime will be commemorated by a rough 'M' cut in the gaol stone near his head.

The cut-down version of the top hat favoured by Franz Müller became fashionable and was thereafter referred to as a 'Müller hat' or 'Müller cut-down'.

CHAPTER 3

Milsom and Fowler
Muswell Hill, 1896

... lying in the sink they found a small, broken lantern with multicoloured bull's-eye glasses.

This case is remarkable for the fact that a toy lantern left at the scene of the crime formed the principal evidence in bringing the culprits to justice. Along with another murderer, Milsom and Fowler were hanged at Newgate, this being the last triple hanging to take place there.

In 1896, the most imposing house in Tetherdown, a thorough-fare leading off Queens Avenue and Fortis Green, in Muswell Hill, was Muswell Lodge, sited at what is today the junction of Tetherdown with Burlington Road. This splendid neo-gothic mansion was situated in extensive grounds on the west side of the street. The main entrance in Tetherdown Lane was protected by a high gate and at the rear was a large garden stretching down to Coldfell Woods.

Muswell Lodge was inhabited by seventy-nine-year-old retired engineer Henry Smith, a widower of twenty-four years, who was a somewhat miserly and reclusive man, who lived alone but was attended by a servant. Despite his advanced years Mr Smith was remarkably strong and fit. He was powerfully built, stood 6 feet tall and weighed 17 stones. He was also very security conscious and took various precautions regarding the protection of his home. Everywhere was locked at night. His gardener had placed several alarms and mantraps throughout the grounds, and an alarm-gun protected the rear of the premises in case anyone attempted to enter from the woods. A gun was linked to a trip wire that was stretched across the full width of the garden and kept in position about 18 inches above the ground by a series of iron staves. Anyone coming into contact with the trip wire would fire the gun.

Charles Webber, of 1 Coppets Road, Mr Smith's gardener for ten years, used to start work as soon as it was light during the winter months and finish at 5.30pm. On the evening of Thursday 13 February 1896, he set the alarm-gun and left the garden at his usual time. At 11.30pm he returned to bank-up the greenhouse fire, and let himself in and out by the side gate. Everything seemed perfectly normal and all was quiet in the house, as Mr Smith usually went to bed around 8.00pm.

On the morning of Friday 14 February, Mr Webber arrived at Muswell Lodge and was surprised to find everything locked – Mr Smith was an early riser and usually unlocked the front gate. As was his normal practice, Mr Webber went to deactivate the alarm-gun. After discovering that it had been tampered with, he went to the house and knocked on the front door. He became increasingly concerned when he could get no reply and proceeded to investigate further. When he looked through the kitchen window he saw something lying on the floor but could not make out what it was. At that point he decided to summon help. First he called on Joseph

The shocking discovery of Henry Smith's body in the kitchen at Muswell Lodge.
Illustrated Police News

Stanbrook, a nurseryman, of 3 Tetherdown. By then the early morning light was waking local residents and some were already out on the streets. Several, including Major George Challen, accompanied Webber and Stanbrook back to Muswell Lodge. They found the sash of the kitchen window was up but the blind was down. The major lifted the blind and discovered the body of Mr Smith on the kitchen floor. When they entered the mansion it was clear that Smith had suffered a violent death. Nothing could be done for him and the police were summoned to the murder scene.

The police noted that Henry Smith was dressed in his white nightshirt. His arms had been tied to his body by a tablecloth, which had been torn into strips. His legs were bound in a similar way. Part of the tablecloth and a towel were wrapped around the victim's head, and some of the towel was forced into his mouth. There were bruises to the head and to the hands as well as various cuts. The kitchen showed signs of a violent struggle, there were too separate pools of blood on the floor, and blood was spattered on the walls. The evidence at the crime scene also suggested that Mr Smith had tried to defend himself. A brace and bit had been left on the kitchen table and lying in the sink they found a small, broken lantern with multicoloured bull's-eye glasses. Two penknives had been left near the body – it was believed they had been used to tear the cloth into strips – and the presence of two knives suggested two people were involved in the crime. Various items of discarded jewellery were found around the house and the still-open safe had been rifled. It was clear to the police that this was a burglary that had gone disastrously wrong. When they examined the grounds they found two sets of footprints near the fence beyond which was Coldfell Woods, clearly the burglar's escape route.

There was extensive press coverage of the case, London's evening papers were the first to break the story when the *Evening News* reported on Friday 14 February:

> Burglary and Murder – old gentleman tied and beaten to death at Muswell Hill

The following day, *The Times* headline read:

> Shocking Murder at Muswell Hill

The post-mortem examination on Henry Smith suggested that he had put up a good fight. His injuries were extensive. He had a black eye, about twelve scalp wounds, cuts to both his hands and a broken finger. His skull had also been fractured. The injuries suggested that Mr Smith's assailant had beaten him with a jemmy. The cause of death was given as concussion and loss of blood.

On Wednesday 19 February, the *Evening News* reported:

> The funeral of Mr Henry Smith, the old gentleman murdered at Muswell Lodge, took place at noon to-day in the Old Cemetery, Highgate. The remains were buried in a private grave, in which are buried his father and mother and his wife, whom he lost twenty years ago after only eighteen months' happyness [sic] of wedded life ... The bearers were eight in number, the coffin being an exceedingly large and heavy one.

The police acted on the premise that they were looking for two men, and the behaviour of two known felons immediately following the crime left the police with few doubts that the pair were indeed the suspects they were looking for. Albert Milsom was thirty-two-years-old and had already been convicted of a long list of crimes, mostly burglary. He had used several aliases including Charles Wilson, James Mead and Charles Smith. He was 5 feet 5 inches tall, had dark brown hair, hazel eyes, a dark complexion and muscular build He was not by nature a violent man. He, his twenty-five-year-old wife Emily and their two children lived at Emily's mother's house, at 133 Southam Street, Kensal Town, an area to the north-east of Kensington and west of Maida Vale, straddling Harrow Road. Emily's fifteen-year-old brother Henry Miller also lived in the house.

Milsom had for some time been associated with another burglar and resident of Kensal Town who also had a long record, but unlike Milsom this man was known to be extremely violent. Henry Fowler, known as Bunny to his friends, was thirty-one-years-old, and he too used various aliases, including Henry Sabard and Thomas Brown. He was a powerfully-built brute of a man and stood 5 feet 10 inches tall. He had dark hair, brown eyes and a mole just above his left nostril. He was released from Dartmoor on parole, on 16 January 1896, having served time for burglary with violence, and was shortly thereafter seen around Kensal Town and Kilburn, with Allbert Milsom. Unbeknown to Fowler, shortly after his release on licence from Dartmoor, a plain-clothes policeman, Police Constable Burrell of the North Kensington force, had been assigned to keep an eye on him. Milsom's renewed association with Fowler had been noted by Burrell.

After their arrest in Bath, on Saturday 10 April, almost eight weeks following the murder, Milsom, aware of the mounting evidence against them, gave his account of events to the police, and much of what follows draws on that statement. Milsom said that at about 8.00pm on the evening of Thursday 13 February, Fowler arrived at his home in Kensal Town and suggested that they do a burglary together. Milsom reported that Fowler said to him:

> I have had a look round with another man who done a lagging with me, and he pointed out several places. There is one place especially where an old man lives. You know how them people are. Any little hole or corner they put their money in. We might find something there. Will you come?

Milsom said that he refused at first, but Fowler persisted in trying to persuade him and in the end he agreed. Fowler said he needed a light. After asking for a candle and being told none was available, he spotted a small lantern on the kitchen dresser. It had three glasses – white, green and red – and was similar to those used by railway guards. In fact it was a toy lantern which belonged to Milsom's brother-in-law, Henry:

> We will take that. It won't throw the reflection so.

said Fowler. The two men went to Kilburn where they drank in a pub with several of Fowler's friends. They then travelled to Muswell Hill, but not before stopping off at another pub. When the two burglars arrived at Muswell Lodge, Fowler climbed over the front gate and Milsom followed him. Fowler warned Milsom to look out for any alarms:

> ... or we shall find ourselves being surrounded by police ...

They then went around to the back of the house where there was a large lawn with a bed in the centre containing shrubs. They lay in the bushes for about an hour, watching and listening for any movement within the house. Satisfied that all was well, Fowler whispered to Milsom:

> We will get to work.

Milsom told the police that they began to search for a way into the house. The drawing-room window was first tried but, despite

Fowler putting all his weight on the jemmy, he had placed under the sash, it would not budge. Next, a small scullery window was tried but that was securely barred. They then tried another window, having first removed the flowerpots from the sill. This time Fowler was successful. He opened the sash, then climbed inside the house. The room was a kitchen. Fowler went to the door that led to the rest of the house. Finding it locked, he took out a brace and bit from the bag he was carrying and began drilling holes around the lock. Unbeknown to Fowler and Milsom, Henry Smith's bedroom was directly above the kitchen. Mr Smith must have heard either Fowler gaining entry or the vibration of the drill because he went to investigate.

Fowler had drilled two holes through the door and was about to start on a third when Milsom warned him that a light was showing under the door and growing brighter; someone was coming down the stairs. Milsom called to Fowler:

Bunny, out you come, there's someone coming.

But Fowler did not come out of the window. The two men heard a key being turned in the lock, and Milsom told the police that at this point he ran to the gate to make his escape, expecting that Fowler would be close behind. Next he heard the shouts of:

Police! Murder!

He stood by the gate and was surprised to see no lights or sound of movement. Having waited a few moments, he then checked the coast was clear before returning to the house. When he reached Muswell Lodge, Fowler stood by the back door covered in blood.

According to Milsom, an angry exchange followed. Fowler blamed Milsom for having left him and cited this as the cause of his attacking Mr Smith. Milsom said Fowler was so angry he was afraid the man would turn his violence on him. Fowler eventually calmed down and, leaving Milsom downstairs, went upstairs to see what he could find. He returned with a watch and chain and some jewellery. However, he decided to leave the jewellery behind 'in case of detection'. He found a key to the safe in Mr Smith's trouser pocket. The safe was opened and rifled. They then left the house and buried their bag of tools in the shrubbery, leaving the back way and clambering over a fence into the woods. They decided to wait in the woods until dawn as Fowler's bloodstained clothes might easily be spotted by police patrols. Three or four hours later they made their way back to the road, emerging from the woods at about 6.00am, into Tetherdown Lane, some way from Muswell Lodge. They then set off for Kensal Town, Fowler wearing Milsom's coat to hide his bloodstained clothing.

When they were almost home Fowler announced that he would go to his brother's place for breakfast and would see him again in a couple of hours. When Milsom arrived home he went straight to bed. At about 10.00am Fowler arrived carrying a parcel containing new clothes. Emily Milsom left the room so he could change into them. He then gave Albert Milsom £50 and said:

> That's more than some would give you after leaving a man in a hole.

Shortly afterwards Fowler went away, leaving his clothes behind for Emily to dispose. The following day, Saturday 15 February, Milsom took Emily and her brother Henry Miller to Harrow Road, where he bought some new clothes home for his brother-in-law and en route they stopped off to buy an outfit for Emily.

On returning to 133 Southam Street, Milsom changed into his new clothes and gave some of his old ones to Henry. When Henry noticed that his lantern had disappeared from the kitchen dresser, he complained bitterly. Milsom told him:

> If anybody asks you about the lantern you are to say you broke it and threw it in the dust hole. It pretty nigh caught us in the fire.

That evening, Albert and Emily Milsom went with Henry Fowler and a lady-friend of his to a concert at a public house in Kilburn. They stayed there until after midnight and Fowler, much the worse for drink, became violent. He was argumentative, picked a quarrel with the woman, punched her and knocked her down. With some difficulty Milsom managed to get a cab and they all returned to Kensal Town where the two couples parted.

On Sunday 16 February, Milsom left home in the morning after telling his wife he would be back for dinner. He went to meet Fowler who told him:

> I'm off. I have got to show myself on the 16th and I don't intend to give my face away.

Fowler was on parole. His licence required him to visit police once a month and that very day he needed to report or he would be returned to prison. Fowler was concerned that he might be on the list of possible suspects for the Muswell Hill murder and was not prepared to take the risk of turning up at the police station only to be arrested. Milsom was also fearful that the police were already hot on their trail. Fowler asked Milsom if he would go abroad with him and Milsom said that he would.

The two men travelled to the East End where they called on Milsom's aunt, Mrs Waddell, at 62 Peter's Street, Mile End. Milsom introduced Fowler to her as Mr Jarvis. Having dined at Mrs Waddell's, Milsom told his aunt he had called on her to say goodbye as he was going abroad. Milsom arranged for his mother, his wife and children to visit him at Mile End. Having promised to write soon, he and Fowler travelled to Euston where they caught a train to Liverpool.

Because the pair had frequently been seen together around Kensal Town and Kilburn since January, their sudden flight attracted even more attention and fleeing was probably their biggest mistake. They certainly did not possess the nous to escape detection for long, and their sudden affluence and unfettered, indiscreet spending power had been noted. Fowler's failure to observe the conditions of his licence on 16 February threw further suspicion on him. While the police investigation into their involvement in the crime was still in its early stages, Milsom and Fowler found lodgings in Liverpool. Milsom wrote to Emily to let her know where he was staying. She sent him a telegram by return informing him that his brother Fred would visit him in Liverpool the following day. Fred handed his brother a sealed letter from Emily which told him that the police had visited their house and were looking for Fowler because he was wanted under the terms of his licence. She also told him that the police knew they had gone off together and that he would get twelve months' for being in Fowler's company. At this stage Emily was not aware of any connection between her husband's disappearance with Fowler and the police investigation into the robbery and murder at Muswell Hill. Fred returned to London and the pair of villains remained in Liverpool. Fowler took one step to try to alter his appearance during his stay there. He had some front teeth missing and this fact appeared in the official police description, so he went to a dentist and had false ones fitted.

Police investigations soon revealed that two men answering the description of Milsom and Fowler had been seen at Euston. A further visit by the police to Milsom's house in Southam Street,

Kensal Town, left no doubt that Milsom and Fowler were the men involved in the Muswell Lodge murder and efforts to find them increased. Officers questioned Emily's brother, Henry Miller. He talked quite freely and told the truth. When he was shown the lantern that had been left at the scene of the crime, Henry identified it as his own. Indeed, he went to great lengths to explain how several marks had appeared on it. He said he had purchased it at the post office in Golborne Road, Kensal Town, shortly before Christmas 1895. He found it did not work properly, so he repaired it himself. The repairs were clearly visible. Henry explained with enthusiasm the modifications he had made and when the lamp was examined his assertions were easily verified by the police, leaving no doubt that this was indeed his lamp. This was to be the most important and damning piece of evidence against Milsom and Fowler.

Henry told the police that the lantern had disappeared on the night of 13 February, and during his long statement he mentioned that his brother-in-law had woken him as he returned home in the early hours of the following day. Having established this important fact, Chief Inspector Marshall, conducted a thorough search of the house. He found some pawn tickets in a teapot. When the items on pawn were redeemed they included a bundle of clothing – Emily had pawned the old clothes Fowler had given her to dispose of and these were the clothes he had worn on the night of the burglary. Among them was a bloodstained jacket. Fortunately for Emily she was not charged with any crime as it was decided that she would not have pawned the bundle of clothes and left the pawn ticket in a teapot where anyone could find it had she been aware of their recent history.

The police were soon hot on the trail of the two men and only just missed them in Liverpool. Fowler, true to his usual form, had proved objectionable to their landlady by taking a woman back to his room. An argument ensued and the result was they were thrown out of their lodgings. Milsom and Fowler spent a night in a hotel before leaving for Cardiff, hoping to secure a passage abroad from there. It proved to be a shrewd move as the police were thrown completely off the scent, but Milsom and Fowler never made their journey overseas.

It was during their stay in Cardiff that an opportunity arose that may explain why they decided to remain. They encountered a showman, in fact a phrenologist – a person who claimed to be able to read another person's character by feeling the bumps on their head. This type of act was a very popular attraction at sideshows, particularly in seaside resorts. He billed himself as 'Professor Sinclair, the Eminent Phrenologist'. Somehow an idea was formulated and Milsom and Fowler, calling themselves Arthur Scott and Henry Taylor, told the professor that they had recently returned from abroad and were looking for a business opportunity to invest in. The idea of some sort of travelling show was discussed.

For a time, Fowler remained on his best behaviour. The professor's run came to an abrupt end in Cardiff. The act was paid off two weeks before the end of the show's projected run as a result of lack of an audience and suggestions of chicanery, but not before Milsom and Fowler had assisted the professor and his wife in the various acts they performed, which included ventriloquism. They clearly felt that this was a way they could make some money and escape detection. It was agreed that if the professor could find another venue, they would split the costs and eventually share the profits. After just four days in Cardiff, Milsom and Fowler, along with Fowler's new lady friend, followed professor Sinclair to Newport, Pontypool and on to Bristol, where the woman left. The travelling show stayed for two weeks in Bristol and one Sunday during this period Milsom went to London to see his wife and children. He returned to the West Country the following day, bringing his family with him. On 30 March, the travelling show moved to Swindon. It had proved an expensive exercise and the pair of would-be impresarios found themselves covering not only their own expenses but the Sinclair's also. As was established during the trial, the money rapidly began to run out and so did Fowler's patience and good humour. His grandiose idea of becoming a strongman in the show had not come to fruition and he soon became abusive and threatening towards Professor and Mrs Sinclair.

In Swindon, Milsom and Fowler made a failed attempt at breaking into a jeweller's shop. On Sunday 5 April, now desperately short of money, they found themselves in Chippenham where they spent the night in the station waiting-room. The following day they moved to Bath, where they lodged near the theatre, above a confectionary and grocery shop kept by Emma Warren at 36 Monmouth Street. Milsom, Emily, their two small children and the Fowlers all shared one room. Fowler found lodgings elsewhere.

Police Constable Burrell had been hard at work since the disappearance of the two burglars on 16 February. The absence of Emily and her children did not go unnoticed, arousing suspicion that they had joined Milsom. After their departure Constable Burrell visited 133 Southam Street and there he discovered an envelope. The postmark enabled him eventually to track the party down. Burrell's investigations took him from town to town, and once he had discovered the existence of Professor Sinclair's travelling show and Milsom and Fowler's involvement in it, his task of discovering their whereabouts became much easier. When the show arrived in Bath on 6 April, Easter Monday, little did the pair know that the police had caught up with them.

Once more, Milsom and Fowler intended to line up a job. To that end they selected yet another jeweller's, Mr Veal's, at 6a Stall Street. While Milsom and Fowler were watching the shop, taking careful note of Mr Veal's movements, the police were watching Milsom and Fowler. On Saturday 10 April, two police officers, Chief Inspector Marshall, of Scotland Yard and Inspector Nutkins, of Kensal Town, travelled to Bath where they joined Police Constable Burrell. A lengthy conference was held with senior local police officers and a plan of action formulated. The following evening the police threw a tight but unobtrusive cordon around 36 Monmouth Street. The officers were given instructions to allow anyone in but nobody out. That evening Milsom was with his wife in their room. At about 11.00pm Fowler arrived. The police were ready to make their move. The raiding party was unusual in that it consisted principally of senior officers – Chief Inspector Marshall, Chief Inspector Noble, Detective Inspector Mountfield, Inspector Newport, Inspector Nutkins and Police Constable Burrell. All carried loaded revolvers.

When the policemen burst into the room they had the advantage of complete surprise. Each officer had been assigned his man and made for him. Inspector Newport rushed for Fowler who resisted and reached for a revolver which was on the mantelpiece. Chief Inspector Marshall was quick to act and brought the butt of his revolver down on the back of Fowler's head. Milsom was apprehended by Inspector Nutkins; he offered no resistance. Everyone in the room was taken into custody. Milsom and Fowler were both charged with murder. Emily Milson with being an accessory after the fact. It became clear that Professor and Mrs Sinclair knew nothing about the real identities of the two men and they were released the following afternoon.

Some of Milsoms's account of the events may have been true, but his claim that he knew nothing of the planned burglary until 13 February is difficult to believe – several residents of Tetherdown claimed to have seen both Milsom and Fowler acting suspiciously in the area the day before the burglary took place. In addition, his account of the crime scene is not exactly consistent with the police evidence. However, the evidence against Milsom and Fowler was so overwhelming that if Milsom did put a slant on the story in his favour it can hardly have altered the outcome of the trial.

Following their arrest in Bath, the prisoners were conveyed to the railway station and placed in a sealed compartment with a police escort. When they arrived at Paddington a large crowd was waiting for them. A crowd had also gathered at Highgate Police Station where the pair were taken immediately after their arrival in London and formally charged. It became clear during their various appearances at Highgate magistrates' court that the police had gathered a considerable amount of evidence against the two men. It was at this point that Milsom, who was being held at Holloway Prison, wrote to Chief Inspector Marshall, offering to confess. Chief Inspector Marshall, accompanied by Inspector Nutkins, went to see Milsom on 28 April, at Holloway, where they heard his lengthy confession. As well as giving a full account of the events, Milsom told the police where he and Fowler had buried their burglars' tools. These were soon found, just as Milsom had said they would be, in the shrubbery, in the back garden at Muswell Lodge. When Fowler heard of Milsom's confession he, too, decided to tell his version of events. Evidence later presented in court recorded that he told a police escort:

My pal, the dirty dog, has turned Queen's evidence and our mouthpiece is no use. But I can tell a tale as well as he. There was £112 in the bag in the safe and I gave him £53 and some shillings, which was an equal share of the money after what I had spent. Is it likely that I should give that to a man who stood outside? He put his foot on the old man's neck until he was sure he was dead and then we went upstairs, he first, and found the old man's trousers with the keys to the safe in the pocket. But thieves will cut one another's throat for half a loaf.

The trial of Albert Milsom and Henry Fowler began at the
Central Criminal Court, Old Bailey, on 19 May 1896, before Mr
Justice Hawkins. C F Gill and Horace Avory appeared for the
crown; Milson was defended by Mr Hutton and Mr Rooth, and
Fowler, by Mr Woodfall and Mr Abinger. The evidence was
heavily stacked against them. In addition to the clue provided by
the toy lantern, this case is notable for the violent outburst that

Henry Fowler attacks Albert Milsom in the dock at the Old Bailey. Illustrated
Police News

came as the jury returned with their guilty verdict. Fowler flung himself across the dock at his accomplice and tried to strangle him, very nearly succeeding in saving the executioner the job of hanging Milsom.

Milsom and Fowler received their sentence of death on 21 May. Both were found to be equally guilty of the crime, although doubts were subsequently expressed about the part Milsom played in the slaying of Henry Smith. He was not a violent man but he was easily led, and in the end that was his downfall. The pair were hanged at Newgate on 10 June 1896, with a Whitechapel murderer called William Seaman. Seaman was convicted of what became known as the Turner Street Murders, the double murder of seventy-seven-year-old John Goodman Levy and his thirty-five-year-old house-keeper, Sarah Gale, at 31 Turner Street, on 4 April 1896. Seaman was positioned between Milsom and Fowler on the drop and his last words were reputed to have been:

This is the first time I've ever been a bloody peacemaker.

The hanging of Milsom, Fowler and Seaman was the last triple execution at Newgate.

On Wednesday 10 June 1896, *The Times* reported:

After hanging an hour the bodies were cut down, and an inquest was subsequently held before Mr S F Langham, the coroner of the City of London, at the Sessions House , in the Old Bailey. The jury, after being sworn, were taken to view the bodies, which were laid out in black coffins in the execution shed. On their way the jurymen had to pass through the corridor in which are buried the bodies of persons previously executed in the gaol, and it was noticed that men were already at work digging the grave which was to receive the bodies of the three culprits. Beyond the marks around the necks caused by the ropes, the corpses of the men presented no indication of the manner of their death. Formal evidence was given by Colonel Milman and Dr Scott, the latter stating that the executions had been carried out satisfactorily, death being instantaneous. The jury returned the usual verdict. The bodies of the men were afterwards buried together in the same grave.

An unusual mishap occurred during the execution. Four warders were in close attendance on the scaffold. One of them obscured Billington's view of his assistant, Warbrick, who was still

The feared triple gallows at Newgate on which William Seaman was hanged between Albert Milsom and Henry Fowler on 9 June 1896. Author's collection

pinioning the feet of one of the prisoners when Billington operated the lever that opened the trap door. The three criminals plummeted to their deaths as Warbrick was catapulted into the pit. Fortunately, the latter heard the bolt beneath him being withdrawn and instinctively grabbed the legs of the man in front of him. He ended up swinging below the feet of the three dead men!

Following the closure of Newgate in 1902 and prior to the gaols demolition, the bodies of those who had been hanged and buried within Newgate's precincts were lifted and re-buried in the City of London Cemetery.

CHAPTER 4

The Strange Case of Dr Hawley Harvey Crippen
Lower Holloway, 1910

Wrapped in a flannelette pyjama jacket was a stinking mass of human flesh, skin, viscera and hair.

Since 1910, when the Crippen Case first hit the headlines, the story of how the little American doctor who had settled in London became a wife murderer and mutilator, has remained high on the public's list of top True Crime stories. In itself the case is not all that much out of the ordinary. What sets this case apart from other similar, although less high-profile murder cases, is basically one simple fact, that Dr Crippen was the first murderer to be caught by wireless telegraphy. Apart from some amusing incidents during his attempted flight, along with his mistress disguised as a boy, there really isn't anything all that exceptional about the case. In recent years the Crippen Case has once again made considerable copy in national newspapers and has been the subject of television programmes, due to some sensational claims; and the case continues to be the focus of re-assessment and re-examination.

In July 2004, a television programme, *The Last Secret of Dr Crippen*, sought to cast some doubt on Crippen's conviction. It was said that two letters written by Cora Crippen (the supposed murder victim) from America were sent to Crippen at Pentonville Prison, but neither he nor his solicitor was given sight of them. The first letter was allegedly posted from Chicago and written the day Crippen was convicted. It was said to have been received by the governor on 25 October. It was signed Belle Elmore Crippen. Part of it read:

> I don't want to be responsible for your demise if I can save you in this way but I will never come forward personally, as I am happy now.

The programme stated that the second letter, dated 22 October and received several days after the first, was passed on to his superiors by the prison governor, who was anxious to find out about its authenticity. The reply came that it had gone to the Home Secretary. The programme stated that:

> ... the Home Secretary, Winston Churchill ... slipped it into his pocket and plainly forgot about it because it was certainly never given to the defence as it should have been.

The documentary also revealed that:

> Newly discovered papers show that they [Crippen's defence team] weren't told of a further discovery. At the same time that Cora tried to remove £600 from their deposit account, she had hired a removal firm to take six trunks away from Hilldrop Crescent to the home of an American music teacher in Bayswater.

The investigation also included some convincing evidence of possible contamination of the remains, which might have resulted in inaccurate assumptions being made at the time. Ten slides of the remains, used for scientific analysis in 1910, have been kept in a cabinet at the Royal London Hospital in Whitechapel Road. Following recent examination of these slides, some startling claims have been made. Firstly, DNA samples taken from the slides do not match with samples taken from descendents of Cora Crippen's close blood relatives; and secondly, the tissue samples on the 1910 slides were not of a female, but of a male. These revelations have resulted in a member of Dr Crippen's family insisting that he was innocent of the crime with which he was both convicted and hanged, and that therefore his remains should be removed from where they lie to this day, in Pentonville Prison and be reburied in the family plot in the USA. However, some experts claim that in the almost one hundred years since the slides were first made from the tissue samples found in the cellar at Hilldrop Crescent, that the tests made upon these slides ninety-nine years later will not provide satisfactory results, as the many individuals who might have handled the slides over the years and the cross-contamination thus caused, would hardly be likely to give accurate results today.

So, as far as Dr Crippen's guilt or innocence is concerned, it is virtually impossible to establish so long after the actual events. Notwithstanding the fact that Cora Crippen might not have been the victim of murder, some human remains were certainly found at

Hilldrop Crescent and if they were not Cora's, they were definitely somebody else's, and they had been placed there during Crippen's occupancy of the house. One theory is, that in order to supplement his income, in an attempt to satisfy his wife's taste for exotic gowns, expensive wigs and jewellery, Dr Crippen carried out illegal abortions; and that the remains were those of a patient whose abortion went seriously wrong has been banded about for some time.

For the purposes of this account, I will stick to the authorised version of events, and will not deviate from the mass of documentary evidence that exists, which I have sifted through at considerable length, nor speculate on improbables and imponderables.

Miss Kunigunde Mackamotzki of Brooklyn, from New York, soon discovered that both her family name, which was of Polish origin, and her first name, which was equally difficult to pronounce, was holding her back from the ambitious life that in her mind she had mapped out for herself, and she took a step which was to have far reaching consequences. In 1889, at the age of seventeen, she decided to change her name to Cora Turner. Soon afterwards, she was offered a job as secretary to a Brooklyn physician. The buxom Miss Turner soon caught the eye of a professional colleague of her employers. He was a widower, and his name was Hawley Harvey Crippen.

Dr Crippen was born in Coldwater, Michigan, in 1862. His father was a dry-goods merchant. In 1887, Crippen married his first wife, Charlotte Bell, in Santiago. The following year a son was born, Otto Hawley Crippen, who was living in Los Angeles at the time of his father's trial in 1910. After less than three years' marriage Charlotte had died of tuberculosis.

Standing just 5 feet 4 inches tall, Dr Hawley Harvey Crippen had piercing blue eyes, which bulged slightly due to an affliction. Compelled to wear thick-lensed glasses, he blinked constantly. Olive-skinned, brunette Cora Turner, had obviously smitten the quietly spoken doctor, and she recognised in him some potential. Cora had already been the mistress of a wealthy stove manufacturer, C C Lincoln, and she was on the lookout for a gentleman who would keep her in the style to which she had become accustomed and to which she felt she was entitled. The diminutive Doctor evidently fitted the bill. Having set her sights on Dr Crippen, Cora proceeded to woo him, and he found her sufficiently alluring to make him forget the sad loss of his wife. They married on 1 September 1892, three months after they had met. The newlyweds went to St Louis, where they stayed for about a year. Afterwards, they set up house in Brooklyn.

Unbeknown to the little doctor, his new wife nurtured aspirations to become a great opera star, but it seems these aspirations far exceeded her talent as a singer. Far from being the stuff that stars are made of, Cora's capabilities would hardly have gained her admittance to the chorus. Still, she was nothing if not ambitious. According to available accounts, her voice, a thin soprano, was described by one commentator, Filson Young, as 'small but of a clear quality'. If Cora's singing voice was not a belter, her speaking voice nonetheless matched her personality: it had an unmistakable New York twang, was loud, vulgar, unsubtle and 'lacking in feminine charm'. Despite these obvious drawbacks, the many friends she later made in England spoke highly of her.

One of Cora Crippen's friends, who knew her well, Dr John H Burroughs, honorary physician to the Music Hall Ladies' Guild, who first met the Crippens in 1902, described her at Crippen's trial as a:

> ... vivacious woman, I should say about thirty years of age, bright and cheerful, a very pleasant woman generally.

Back in 1892, as the Crippens settled down to married life, Cora decided it was time for her to make her mark on the world of entertainment. She had every confidence in her abilities as a performer. She was determined to be a success and practiced scales day and night. His wife's proclivities for a musical career was only the start of Crippen's troubles. Evidence in his own account of their relationship and reports proffered by friends, family and acquaintances indicates that, following their marriage, Crippen lavished attention on Cora and out of love resolved to do everything he could to further his wife's musical ambitions. Crippen was soon spending large amounts on vocal coaches, and promises of work by theatrical agents spurred Cora on.

For over two years Dr Crippen shelled out considerable sums of money to finance his wife's singing career, and she had yet to earn her first pay cheque as a singer. Despite this heavy burden on his purse strings, the doctor did not wish to dampen his wife's enthusiasm, but her efforts to become a great opera star were emptying his pockets faster than he could fill them. When Dr Crippen secured a new position as a medical expert for a patent medicine company in St Louis, he probably thought a move from the bright lights of New York to a more sedate Missouri, would result in a reduction in his wife's enthusiasm for a musical career. How wrong he was. Not only were bills from vocal coaches soon being presented but Cora began having lavish gowns created by expensive costumiers. With increasing costs ever depleting his finances, Dr Crippen shifted his base of operations and met with greater success in Toronto, Salt Lake City and Philadelphia.

Early in the marriage, Cora Crippen underwent an ovariectomy. This operation left her unable to have children. At twenty-eight and yet to appear on the professional stage, she was beginning to show signs of the character traits that would become the mainstay of her future married life with Crippen. She became frustrated and the once outwardly loving wife, as a result of the inner turmoil her lack of professional success on the stage was causing her, changed her attitude and she began to quarrel with her husband, to criticise and find fault with him at every opportunity. Filson Young, who compiled the Crippen volume for the well-respected *Notable British Trials* series in 1920, said that at this stage the doctor was undoubtedly still fond of his wife, kind to her, patient with her extravagances and the 'interminable calls which she made upon his time and his means'.

Cora decided to change her name for the momentous occasion of her first professional theatrical engagement and she became Macka Motzki. Unfortunately this milestone in her professional career also coincided with a physical change in her appearance. Her ballooning figure led to her being dubbed 'the Brooklyn Matzos Ball'. Her first stage name proved to be short lived and she soon changed it to Belle Elmore.

In 1898, an offer of employment in an entirely new area came Dr Crippen's way and he was overjoyed. The little doctor was thrilled at the exciting prospects that lay before him and he jumped at the chance of moving to London for Munyon's remedies, another patent medicine outfit, on a salary of £3 a week, plus commission. Crippen travelled to London in April. In August, his wife joined him in rooms in South Crescent. They later moved to Guildford Street, before settling at 37 Store Street, off Tottenham Court Road, Bloomsbury. Doctor in name only, his professional qualifications did not allow him to practice in England, but he knuckled down to work that amounted to little more than that of a glorified salesman. Cora, meanwhile, was too busy with her own plans to worry about those less ambitious strivings of her husband. She had other things to concern herself with; she felt sure that music hall, to her mind a far more sophisticated and superior art form than was to be found in the vaudeville and burlesque theatres in her native United States, would give her the chance she needed to shine, and she threw herself into her quest. However, Belle Elmore never achieved more than the occasional music hall or smoking concert engagement.

She did, however, secure some periods of regular employment, which meant that sometimes she was away from home for short periods or even several weeks. At some of her last appearances on stage during an artistes' strike, she was hissed and booed off the stage at the Bedford Music Hall, Camden Town, and the Euston Palace, for being a blackleg. On the same bill at the Euston Palace was an actor named Weldon Atherstone, who received a similar reception and was able to sympathise with the weeping Belle. Three years later, in July 1910, in the same week that Belle Elmore's remains were found at Hilldrop Crescent, Atherstone was found shot dead in the garden of a flat in Battersea. The coincidence was commented upon by Dartford Thomas, the coroner, who a week later was himself dead.

It seems Cora Crippen could not come to terms with the fact that, far from being on the road to becoming a great opera star, her own abilities would not even gain entry into the chorus. Her frustrations knew no bounds and evidence suggests that at this point she began to shut her husband out when it came to activities in the bedroom. As Dr Crippen latter commented, 'she no longer cared for me'.

Crippen was called to Philadelphia for six months on business and during his absence Cora allowed American performer and ex-prizefighter Bruce Miller into her bed. Then, in September 1905, the Crippens moved from their one-bedroom flat in Store Street to a large semi-detached house in Holloway, North London, where they rented 39 Hilldrop Crescent for £52 10s a year from Frederick Lown, of 12 Ashbrook Road, Highgate.

Situated off Camden Road, Hilldrop Crescent is just a few hundred yards from Holloway Prison and less than a mile from Pentonville Prison, which was to feature significantly in the Crippen case. To supplement their income, the Crippens took in paying guests, first German students, then mostly theatrical and variety artistes. This gave Cora the money she needed for her

No 39 Hilldrop Crescent. Author's collection

lavish costumes and blonde wigs. Too lady-like and grandiose to look after the boarders herself, and too mean to employ a maid for the purpose (although the Crippens made use of a charlady occasionally), Cora insisted that her husband get up at the crack of dawn to do the chores. Before he went to his office, the little doctor would go to the kitchen, take up the ashes, black the fire grate, then light the fire. He made the tea, cooked the breakfast and polished the paying guests' boots. Reports say that Cora behaved abominably towards her husband, belittling him in front of the lodgers and flirting lasciviously with other men, some of whom she took to her bed. Cora Crippen was undoubtedly a domineering individual, at least as far as her husband was concerned. She even chose his clothing for him, right down to his underwear. One delivery of clothing to the Crippen household in January 1909 was carefully documented. Jones Brothers of Holloway delivered three suits of pyjamas to 39 Hilldrop Crescent. These pyjamas were to feature prominently in the events that followed.

If Cora Crippen, in the persona of Belle Elmore, had not achieved the degree of success she had hope for on the stage, in off-stage theatrical activities she was becoming something of a personality. She was appointed Honorary Treasurer of the Music Hall Ladies' Guild, and she was mixing with the great and good of the theatrical establishment and furthermore she was liked and respected. However, this exalted position she occupied meant that she was constantly entertaining and this, coupled with her expensive tastes in gowns, further depleted the Crippens' finances. She was particularly adamant in the choice of colour for both her clothes and the décor of their home. She hated the colour green and considered it unlucky, which was not unusual in theatrical circles. However, her dislike went a step further than theatrical superstition. If she were invited into a room decorated green, she invariably made an excuse and left. Pink was her 'lucky' colour and many of the rooms in Hilldrop Crescent were not only decorated but also draped and upholstered in it.

Some of the most famous music-hall artistes of the day often visited Belle Elmore and her husband at Hilldrop Crescent, including Marie Lloyd (1870–1922), the idol of British music-hall audiences. She referred to Crippen as the 'half-a-crown-king' because he habitually invited people out for a drink and then conveniently remembered he had come out without any money. Vesta Tilley, the celebrated beauty who was best known for her male impersonations, was also a regular visitor. Cora was also most likely impressed by the fact that her talented friend, who made several songs famous, including, *Following in Father's Footsteps* and *Jolly Good Luck to the Girl who Loves a Soldier*, had a title, Vesta being in fact Lady de Freece (1864–1952).

It seems Crippen was now expected to act as stand-in whenever his wife was without an admirer, and it has been suggested in various quarters that he took to staying her passion with hyoscine, a poisonous drug used as a nerve depressant and hypnotic. However, only one record has ever been found related to the little doctor purchasing that particular drug and that was shortly before his wife's supposed death.

On the top floor of his home in Hilldrop Crescent the doctor created a peaceful haven to which he could retreat. He would occasionally go out of the house to relax over a drink at the nearby *Admiral Mann* public house, situated in Hargrave Place. He didn't smoke because it made him ill, and wines and spirits affected his heart and digestion, but he was a moderate drinker and enjoyed light ale and stout. In his study or den he would read, write and relax during the precious moments he could escape from the hustle and bustle elsewhere in the house.

It may be that at this time he became interested in the works of William Le Quex, an English novelist, diplomat and pioneer broadcaster who specialised in writing mysteries. The only account of a relationship between the two men came from Le Quex's own contribution to a book entitled *Famous Crimes of Recent Times* and exactly how much truth lies behind it is a matter of conjecture. He was not called as a witness at the trial and I have been unable to find any reference to him in the extensive files released on the Crippen case in 1986. However, in *Famous Crimes of Recent Times*, Le Quex claims that Crippen wrote to him in March 1908, at the *Devonshire Club*, and requested an appointment. He used the assumed name, Dr Adams:

Dear Sir,
I have on several occasions read with interest the novels you have written concerning secret poisoning. I, too, take a great interest in the detection of poisons, and perhaps in some little way my knowledge would be helpful to you. Indeed, I have in my mind a new and exciting plot which you could probably use, and I would much like to meet you and discuss it. If you will kindly make an appointment I shall be delighted to keep it.

Le Quex was due to visit Egypt, but after his return to England some three months later, he arranged to see 'Dr Adams' at the *Devonshire Club*. Crippen apparently poured compliments over the author and eventually got onto the subject of poisons; he asked Le Quex if he could secure him a copy of *Secrets of the State of Venice*, a book on poisons that the novelist had referred to in one of his works. Le Quex told Crippen that he owned a copy, having purchased it in a second-hand bookshop in Stockholm, and would have been happy to lend it, but unfortunately it was in his study in Italy. Le Quex also wrote in his account of the meeting that Crippen seemed to know by heart the *Manual*, by Dr Rudolph August Witthaus, an American toxicologist, whose conclusions were generally accepted as standard. Le Quex wrote:

> It was then he unfolded a most ingenious plot for a new novel, which turned on an undiscovered murder. He had weighed every detail and taken every precaution, so that there was no flaw by which the assassin could be traced. The whole story, as he conceived it, was far too grim and ghastly, and I told him so. He laughed. 'You ought to show the public how easy it is for a clever man to commit murder and go scot-free.' We met several times afterwards, and he outlined other plots, all of them dealing with the adventures of a poisoner. A little later I went to live in Italy and our correspondence ceased.

In *Famous Crimes of Recent Times*, Le Quex's only other reference to his involvement in the case states:

> About a year afterwards, on July 22nd, 1910, I opened an illustrated paper, and there saw the photograph of the visitor who had called himself Dr Adams. But beneath the picture was the name 'Dr Hawley Harvey Crippen', and a warrant was out against him for the murder of his wife.

In September 1908, Crippen secured two part-time jobs, while still continuing his association with Munyon's. Both were paid on a commission basis. One involved the sale of ear trumpets, the other was a contract with a dental company that manufactured false teeth. Yale Tooth Specialists was a large concern with offices in Albion House, 61 New Oxford Street, so he moved there from his premises in Shaftesbury Avenue. Coincidentally, The Music Hall Ladies' Guild also had its offices at Albion House. A secretary was placed at his disposal. Crippen had met the young lady some time previously, when he had been working for the Drouet Institute. Miss Ethel Le Neve originated from Diss in Norfolk, but she completed her education in London when her family moved there. In her own account, *Ethel Le Neve: Her Life Story*, written shortly after her trial and published before Crippen's execution, she recalled:

> One of our intimate friends happened to be a short-hand teacher, and it pleased to give lessons both to my sister and to myself in stenography and typewriting. When my sister was proficient as a shorthand-typist she obtained an engagement at the Drouet Institute. Here I joined her. Very soon afterwards came Dr Crippen, who was fated to influence my life so strangely.
>
> For some reason the doctor took kindly to us, and almost from the first we were good friends. But really he was very considerate to everybody. I quickly discovered that Dr Crippen was leading a somewhat isolated life. I did not know whether he was married or not. Certainly he never spoke about his wife, but one day a friend of his called at the office. My sister and I were taking tea with the doctor, which we ourselves had prepared. 'I wish I had someone to make tea for me,' said the friend. Whereupon the doctor, with his customary geniality, pressed him to stay, and during the chat over the tea-cups mention was made of the doctor's wife.
>
> When the friend had gone my sister asked the doctor whether he was really married. 'It would take the lawyers all their time to find out,' was the mysterious reply. That was all he said.
>
> When my sister left to get married I took her place as Dr Crippen's private secretary. With her departure I felt very lonely. Dr Crippen, too, was very lonely, and our friendship deepened almost inevitably.

Other accounts are vague about Ethel Le Neve's early association with the little doctor, but it seems she remained Crippen's secretary at Albion House. Ethel was tiny, dark, attractive, demure and genteel – almost the exact opposite of what Cora Crippen had become. She lived in lodgings, at 80 Constantine Road, Hampstead, where her landlady was Mrs Jackson. It seems Miss Le Neve and Dr Crippen found that they were soulmates and fell deeply in love, a love cemented in a series of rooms in cheap hotels around Bloomsbury and King's Cross. The relationship was common knowledge among the Crippens' friends and acquaintances. When Cora found out she was outraged. She ridiculed the relationship, just as she had for years ridiculed her husband, cheapening it into something absurd. However, when she found out that Ethel was pregnant, it put an entirely different complexion on the matter. Unable to have children herself, she did not like the idea of another woman bearing her husband's offspring. She threatened to leave Crippen and to live with one of her gentlemen friends. She also threatened to take what she referred to as all 'her' money with her. This much Crippen gave in evidence during his trial. Most of their money, some £600, was held in a joint bank account in the Charing Cross Bank, 128 Bedford Street, Strand. On 15 December 1909, Cora gave twelve months' notice to the bank of the withdrawal of the entire amount, but when Ethel suffered a miscarriage, Cora decided to stay with her husband.

One evening in January 1910 Crippen made a rare appearance at one of Cora's social gatherings. Belle (as she preferred to be called on such occasions) was on good form. Lil Hawthorne, one of her variety performer friends, was there. She said that Belle took her on one side with Dr Crippen and told her that 'Harvey and I have decided to start life all over again. We've both done things we're sorry for, but that's all in the past, isn't it dear?'

By this point in time Ethel had been Crippen's mistress for three years. She was twenty-seven, he was forty-eight. Cora Crippen was thirty-five. On 17 January, Crippen went to the chemists Lewis & Burrows, at 108 New Oxford Street and asked for five grains of hyoscine hydrobromide. This powerful drug came in the form of small, soluble crystals. Lewis and Burrows did not have such a substantial quantity in stock but told Crippen that they would order it for him from their wholesalers, the British Drug House. Crippen duly placed the order in the name of Munyon's Remedies and recorded the planned use for the drug in the Poison Register as 'homeopathic preparation'.

The last people to see Cora Crippen alive were Mr and Mrs Paul Martinetti. Paul and Clara Martinetti were retired music-hall artistes. They were invited to the house in Hilldrop Crescent on the evening of 31 January 1910, and the little dinner party broke up about 1.30am. Paul Martinetti was in ill health and on the evening of the dinner party Cora was suffering from a slight cold. As the Martinettis left the house Clara said: 'Don't come down, Belle. You'll catch a cold.' Cora waved them goodbye from an upstairs window. Other than Dr Crippen himself, that was the last time anyone saw Cora alive. By this time the lodgers had left the house and had not been replaced. Crippen called on the Martinettis the following day at their flat to see how Paul was. Their conversation was relayed at the trial:

How is Belle?

enquired Clara Martinetti.

Oh, she's alright,

came the reply.

Exactly what happened after the Martinettis left 39 Hilldrop Crescent will never be known. Crippen said that he and Cora had a blazing row after she criticized him for not escorting the ill Paul Martinetti upstairs to the lavatory. During his trial he said that his wife told him:

This is the finish of it – I won't stand it any longer – I shall leave you tomorrow and you will never hear of me again.

Crippen also told the police that his wife said he should arrange to cover up any scandal with their mutual friends and the Guild the best way he could.

At his trial Crippen denied murdering his wife, and he lied persistently, variously and hopelessly about what had become of her until the day he died. Even after he had been found guilty of murder he never confessed. After the verdict had been pronounced and he had been sentenced to death, he said:

I still protest my innocence.

However, the evidence against him was overwhelming: the remains found in the cellar at 39 Hilldrop Crescent seemed to be beyond reasonable doubt those of Cora Crippen.

It will never be known whether it was the drug hyoscine that actually killed Cora. The toxicological tests carried out on her remains showed a sufficient amount to have killed her, and poisoning by hyoscine was given as the cause of death. If hyoscine had been administered merely to stifle Cora's sexual appetite, perhaps Crippen accidentally gave her an overdose. Perhaps Cora took the poison herself in the belief that it was a sleeping draught, or perhaps Crippen simply gave his wife the poison disguised in a drink or food and waited for it to take effect. Taken orally, the hyoscine would have caused delirium, then drowsiness, leading to unconsciousness within an hour, then paralysis and within twelve hours, death. Assuming that the little doctor did administer hyoscine to Cora in some way, resulting in her death, the corpse was decapitated, dismembered and filleted. Crippen then set about covering up his wife's disappearance. On the afternoon of 2 February, Cora failed to appear at a meeting of the Music Hall Ladies' Guild, held in a room at Albion House. That morning Crippen had gone to his office and dictated two letters, which were delivered by hand by Ethel Le Neve, and both were signed 'Belle Elmore'. Neither was in Cora Crippen's handwriting, much to the consternation of the ladies of the Guild. The letters said that she was resigning her membership of the Guild, owing to an urgent visit to America due to a family illness. Cora had apparently been too busy getting ready to go to write the letters herself.

On the day the letters were delivered to the Music Hall Ladies' Guild, Crippen pawned some of his wife's jewellery at Attenborough's, of 142 Oxford Street. He did the same on 9 February. The jewellery was pawned for a total of £195, which amounted to more than his annual salary from Munyon's. Lil Hawthorne, Belle Elmore's friend, was on a tour of the provinces when the resignation letter arrived at the Guild. When she returned she wanted more details and went to see Crippen. Lil Hawthorne commented that Belle had left rather suddenly. Crippen informed her that it wasn't a relative of Belle's who was ill but a relative of his. He said the relative lived in San Franciso and that there was quite a lot of money involved, so they had to protect their interests. Naturally, one of them had to go and as he couldn't, so Belle went instead.

On 26 February, Crippen took Ethel Le Neve to the Music Hall Ladies' Guild annual ball at the Criterion – tickets cost half a guinea each. At that point Cora's friends began to take a little more interest in the little doctor. Ethel was wearing one of Cora's brooches, something she mentioned in her own account of what happened in *Ethel Le Neve Her Life Story*:

> When we had discussed the departure of Belle Elmore the doctor thrust his hand into his pocket and drew out a handful of jewels – the jewels which have figured so much in this case. 'Look here,' he said, 'you had better have these. At all events, I wish you would please me by taking one or two. These are good and I should like to know you have some good jewellery. They will be useful when we are dining out, and you will please me if you will accept them. I said, 'Well, if you really wish it, I will have one or two. Pick out

which you like. You know my tastes.' Thereupon he picked out a couple of solitaire rings, a ring set with four diamonds and a ruby, and a small diamond brooch – 'the rising sun' brooch. There remained a very large brooch set with beautiful stones in the shape of a tiara, with many rows of diamonds arranged in a crescent, and about half a dozen fine rings.

I think I might say here that Dr Crippen was a real expert in diamonds. He often used to show me how to know the relative values of them by holding them up to the light and watching their colour. As a result I got to know the different fashions of setting, and could distinguish between those set in London and New York.

I then asked what he would do with the remainder, as it would not do to leave them about the house, and as we had no safe, surely it would be better to either sell them or to pawn them. Perhaps the latter course would be best, as he could redeem them whenever he was disposed to do so. 'That is a good idea,' he said. 'I will take your advice.'

It will be seen, therefore, that Dr Crippen pawned the jewels purely on my suggestion. As far as I know, at that time he was not in financial trouble, tempting him to pawn those jewels immediately, as was suggested in court. After all, as regards the jewels they had been bought by Dr Crippen as an investment. It was impossible for Belle Elmore to have paid for them. I have seen her contracts, and I know that even when engaged on tour her salary amounted at most to £3 a week, out of which she had to pay her agent's fee and other expenses. How, then, could she have bought jewels worth many hundreds of pounds? And if the property were not hers why should she take it away?

At the ball, neither 'the rising sun' brooch nor the relationship between the doctor and his secretary escaped the scandalised eyes and the gossiping tongues of the ladies of the Guild. Belle's friends were puzzled that they hadn't heard from her, not even a postcard. When one committee member of the Guild, Louise Smythson, asked Crippen for his wife's address, he told her that she was 'right up in the wilds of the mountains of California'. She then said to him: 'When you get to hear of her will you let us know?' Crippen answered: 'Yes, when she has a settled address I will let you know.' On Saturday 12 March 1910, Ethel moved into 39 Hilldrop Crescent, posing as a housekeeper. A French maid was later engaged – they brought her back from France after visiting Boulogne that Whitsuntide. She was called Valentine and was seventeen years old.

Mrs Jackson, Ethel's landlady, told the court at Crippen's trial that Le Neve had been 'much depressed and in tears in January'. 'It's Miss Elmore,' Ethel informed Mr Jackson. 'When I see them go away together it makes me realise what my position is.' Ethel also confided in her landlady. 'She's been threatening to go away and when she does, the doctor's going to divorce her and marry me.' Before leaving her lodgings (she had spent little time there in the preceding weeks) she informed Mrs Jackson that Mrs Crippen had gone to America.

After her arrival at the house in Hilldrop Crescent, Ethel was seen in Holloway and district wearing clothes and furs that had belonged to Cora Crippen. On Wednesday 16 March, Crippen gave his landlord three months' notice of his intention to vacate the house. Having still not heard from Belle, her friends asked Crippen for news. He told them his wife had developed pneumonia in California and was dangerously ill. Then on 24 March, the little doctor and his mistress went on a five-day Easter holiday to Dieppe as Mr and Mrs Crippen. Before they left Crippen sent a telegram to the Martinettis saying: 'Belle died yesterday at six o'clock. Peter.' (To most of Belle Elmore's theatrical friends her husband was known as Peter – a name she sometimes called him too.) Crippen also took out a death notice in *The Era* on 26 March. Printed on page 17, it simply read:

ELMORE – March 23, in California, U.S.A.
Miss Belle Elmore (Mrs H. H. Crippen)

The same publication, read widely by music-hall and variety artistes, printed an obituary and details of the case on 23 July.

On their return from France, Crippen continued with his sub-terfuge as Cora's friends bombarded him with questions. 'She passed on of pneumonia, up in the high mountains of California,' he told them. Requests for details of where flowers could be sent were answered with: 'There was no point in sending flowers as the funeral had already taken place.' Crippen said that his wife had been cremated and her ashes would be sent to him in England. He had perhaps underestimated his wife's popularity. Cora's friends would not let the matter rest, particularly when it was discovered that on her arrival in America she had not made contact with any of her acquaintances in New York. Meanwhile, Crippen continued to administer his business affairs as usual and on 18 June he arranged with his landlord to stay on until 29 September at Hilldrop Crescent.

However, Lil Hawthorne, widely known as a busybody, was not satisfied. She continued to pester Crippen because, she said, she wanted to pay her respects to her dear friend. He told her he was still awaiting Cora's ashes, but she did not believe him. Lil Hawthorne was not the type of woman to be put off easily; she smelled a rat and she was one of the chief instigators of a move amongst Belle Elmore's friends to ensure the authorities looked into the situation. A friend of one of the members of the Music Hall Ladies' Guild happened to be Detective Superintendent Froest of Scotland Yard. He was in charge of the recently formed serious crime squad. The suspicion that something was not quite right regarding the disappearance of the Music Hall Ladies' Guild's former treasurer, was communicated to Froest and he promised to look into the matter. Detective Chief Inspector Walter Dew was assigned to make general enquiries.

Dew and Detective Sergeant Mitchell visited 39 Hilldrop Crescent on 8 July. The doctor was not a home; only Ethel and the French maid were at the house. Ethel told the two policemen that Dr Crippen was at his office and she agreed to accompany them to Albion House. When they arrived Dew explained the reason for the visit and Crippen said:

I suppose I'd better tell the truth.

This was a quote Dew later reported in his autobiography. A statement was taken over the course of five hours. Crippen said that by the time he came home from work on 1 February his wife had gone. She had run off with another man. To add insult to injury she had left most of her clothes and the jewels he had given her, and left him with no clue as to her whereabouts. Realising she had finally left him, he had sat down to think how he could explain his wife's disappearance without causing a scandal, and conceal the fact that he had been cuckolded.

Crippen's statement read:

I am forty-eight years of age. After being questioned by Chief Inspector Dew as to the statements made by me that my wife, known as Belle Elmore, is dead. I desire to make a voluntary statement to clear the whole matter up. I was born at Coldwater, Michigan, U.S.A., in the year 1862, my father's name being Myron Augustus Crippen, a dry goods merchant. My mother's name was Ardessee Crippen, nee Skinner. My mother is now dead, but my father lives at Los Angeles, California.

It was about 1893, while with Dr Jeffery, that I met Belle Elmore, who was being attended by him. Her name at that time was Cora Turner. I forget where she was living but she was living alone. She was about seventeen years of age, and I, of course, about thirty. She, at the time, was living under the protection of a man named C C Lincoln, a stove manufacturer, of New York. She had been living with him, but he had given up his house and had taken a room for her and was paying all her expenses. I took her to several places for some weeks, as I was very fond of her, and one day she told me Lincoln wanted her to go away with him. I told her I could not stand that, and would marry her right away.

A few days after I married her at a minister's house at Jersey City. Some little time after she told me her name was not Turner, but Kunigunde Mackamotski. She said that her mother, who had been dead some years, was married twice. Her father was a Russian Pole and her mother was a German. Her step-father, so far as I know, is still living, and resides at Forest Avenue, Brooklyn. Her parents were in rather ordinary circumstances, but she had a good education and spoke German well. Afterwards I went to St Louis, and acted as consulting physician to an optician. From there I went to New York, and took up a position with the Munyon Remedy Company.

I was there some time, and while there, about 1899, my wife, who had a good voice, went to New York to have her voice trained, as she thought of going in for grand opera. I paid all her expenses and occasionally visited her at New York. In 1900, or thereabouts, I came to England alone, where I was manager for Munyon's at their offices in Shaftesbury Avenue, and I lived at Queen's Road, St John's Wood. It was in April when I came over, and she joined me in August, as she wrote and told me she was giving up her lessons in grand opera and was going in for music hall sketches. To this I objected, and told her to come over here. She came, and we went to live in South Crescent.

When she came to England she decided to give sketches on the music hall stage, and adopted the name Macke Motzke, but she did not make anything at it. She gave a sketch at the old

Marylebone Music Hall, but it was a failure, and she gave it up. After this she did not do anything for two or three years, until I had to go to America about two years after coming here. My firm sent for me, and I became manager in Philadelphia. When I left England my wife and I were living in Guildford Street, and she remained there while I was away. I remained in Philadelphia from November until the following June, and sent my wife money regularly.

When I returned I found she had been singing at smoking concerts for payment, and that an American music hall artist named Bruce Miller had been a frequent visitor at her house. She told me that this man had visited her, had taken her about, and was very fond of her; also she was very fond of him. I may say that when she came to England from America her manner towards me entirely changed. She had cultivated a most ungovernable temper, and seemed to think I was not good enough for her. She boasted of the men of good position travelling on the boat who had made a fuss of her, and indeed some of them had visited her at South Crescent, but I do not know their names. I never saw the man Bruce Miller, but he used to call when I was out, and take her out in the evening. I did not think anything of Bruce Miller visiting my wife at the time.

It was in 1905, I think, that we removed to 39, Hilldrop Crescent, for which I paid £50 a year. It is quite four years since she ever went out to sing at all, and although we apparently lived very happily together as a matter of fact there were very frequent occasions when she got into most violent tempers, and often threatened she would leave me, saying she had a man she could go to, and that she would end it all. I have seen letters from Bruce Miller to her, which ended with 'love and kisses to brown eyes'.

About four years ago, in consequence of these frequent outbursts, I discontinued occupying her room, and have never cohabited with her since. She did all the housework herself with the exception of having a charwoman in occasionally. About two years ago she became hon. Treasurer to the Music Hall Ladies' Guild, and was there every Wednesday. I never interfered with her movements in any way. She went in and out just as she liked and did what she liked. It was of no interest to me. As I say, she frequently threatened to leave me, and said that if she did she would go right out of my life, and I should never see or hear of her again.

On Monday night, the day before I wrote the letter to the guild resigning her position as treasurer, Mr and Mrs Paul Martinetti came to our place to dinner. After they had left my wife abused me for not paying more attention, and said: 'This is the finish of it. I won't stand it any longer. I shall leave you tomorrow, and you will never hear of me again.' She had said this so often that I did not take much notice of it, but she did say one thing which she had never said before, namely, that I was to arrange to cover up any scandal with our mutual friends and the guild the best way I could. Before this she had told me frequently that the man she would go to was better able to support her than I was. I came to business next morning, and when I went home between 5.00 or 6.00pm. I found she had gone.

Then I realised that she had gone, and I sat down to think it over as to how to cover up her absence without ant scandal. I think the same night, or the next morning (Wednesday), I wrote a letter to the guild saying she had gone away, which I also told several people. I afterwards realised that this would not be a sufficient explanation for her not coming back, and later on I told people that she was ill with bronchitis and pneumonia, and afterwards I told them that she was dead from this ailment. I told them she died in California, but I have no recollection of telling anyone exactly where she died. Someone afterwards asked me where my son lived, and I told them.

I then put an advertisement in the *Era* that she was dead, as I thought that this would prevent people asking me a lot of questions. Whatever I said to other people in regard to her death is absolutely wrong, and I am giving this an explanation. So far as I know she did not die, but is still alive. It is not true that she went away on legal business for me or to see any relations in America. I did not receive any cables to say that she was ill, and it is not true that she was cremated at San Franciso, and that the ashes were sent to me, or that she sailed for Havre.

Everything I have told you is true. I do not know what clothing, if any, she took away. Whenever she quarrelled and she threatened to leave me, she told me she wanted nothing from me. I bought all her jewellery, and, so far as I know, she never had any jewellery given to her. I do not know that she ever had any money sent to her, except that Bruce Miller used to send her small amounts on her birthday and at Easter and Christmas to purchase a present. She suffered from bilious attacks, and I have given her medicine for that – homeopathic remedys [sic]. It is true that I was at the Benevolent Fund dinner at the Criterion with Miss Le Neve, and she wore the brooch my wife left behind. She has also worn my wife's furs.

Miss Le Neve has been in my employ, and was known to me through being employed by the firms for whom I worked for the past eight years. She is now living with me as my wife at Hilldrop Crescent. I have been intimate with her during the past three years. I have frequently stayed with her at hotels, but was never away from home at night.

After I told people my wife was dead, Miss Le Neve and I went to Dieppe for about five days, and stayed at an hotel there. My belief is that my wife has gone to Chicago to join Bruce Miller, whose business on the music hall stage is a musical instrument turn.

Ethel Le Neve made the following statement:

I am a single woman, twenty-seven, years of age, and am a short-hand typist. My father and mother reside at 17b, Goldington Buildings, Great College Street, Camden Town. My father is a commercial traveller. Since the latter end of February I have been living at 39, Hilldrop Crescent with Dr Crippen as his wife. Before this I lived at 30 Constantine Road, Hampstead. I have been on intimate terms with Mr [sic] Crippen for two or three years, but I have known him for ten years. I made his acquaintance by being in the same employment as he was. I knew Mrs Crippen, and have visited Hilldrop Crescent. She treated me as a friend.

In the early part of February I received a note from Mr Crippen saying Mrs Crippen had gone to America, and asking me to hand over a packet he enclosed to Miss May. About 4.00pm the same day he came to our business place, Albion House, and told me his wife had gone to America. He said she had packed up and gone. I had been in the habit for the past two or three years of going about with him, and continued doing so.

About a week after he had told me she had gone to America. I went to Hilldrop Crescent to put the place straight, as there were no servants kept, but at night I went to my lodgings. I did this daily for about a fortnight. The place appeared to be all right and quite as usual. He took me to the Benevolent Fund dinner and lent me a diamond brooch to wear.

Later on he told me I could keep it. After this he told me she had caught a chill on board the ship and had got pneumonia. Afterwards he told me she was dead. He told me he could not go to the funeral as it was too far, and she would have been buried before he got there. Before he ever told me this I had been away with him for five of six days at Dieppe, and stayed at a hotel with him in the names of Mr and Mrs Crippen. When we came back he took me to Hilldrop Crescent, and I remained there with him. The same night, or the night after, he told me that Belle was dead. I was very much astonished, but I don't think I said anything to him about it. I have not had any conversation with him about it since. He gave me some furs of his wife to wear, and I have been living with him ever since as his wife. My father and mother do not know what I am doing, and think I am housekeeper at Hilldrop Crescent. When Mr Crippen told me his wife had gone to America, I don't remember if he told me she was coming back or not. I cannot remember if he went into mourning.

After the statements had been taken, the doctor and Ethel accompanied the two policemen to Hilldrop Crescent, where Crippen allowed them to look around. They searched the house from top to bottom, including the coal cellar, and were satisfied nothing was amiss. Crippen must have felt uneasy about this police attention, because at this point he panicked and fled with Ethel to Rotterdam.

On Monday 11 July, Chief Inspector Dew returned to Albion House to clear up some final points. Crippen was not at his office. However, his associate, Dr Rylance, informed the inspector that on the previous Saturday he had received a letter from Crippen instructing him to wind up his business affairs and household accounts. Included in the letter was the sentence:

In order to escape trouble I shall be obliged to absence myself for a time . . .

A dental technician employed at Albion House, William Long, told Dew that Crippen had sent him out to purchase clothing for a boy of sixteen, and he had gone out and bought a brown tweed suit, stockings, boots, hat and overcoat.

When the inspector visited 39 Hilldrop Crescent, he discovered that the only occupant was the French maid, Valentine. It was clear that further investigation would be required. The house was searched from top to bottom once again and a third time during the following two days. On first inspection, the coal cellar seemed to be perfectly in order. Even after a second inspection, nothing appeared to be amiss. It was only when Dew prodded the cellar floor with a poker that he discovered some of the bricks were loose. Dew and Detective Sergeant Mitchell removed them. There was evidence that the earth beneath had recently been disturbed and the presence of lime encouraged them to dig deeper. It was not long before what little remained of Cora Crippen was found at a depth of 5 inches. Wrapped in a flannelette pyjama jacket was a stinking mass of human flesh, skin, viscera and hair (some of it attached to a Hinde's curler). There was also part of a tattered handkerchief and a cotton camisole. The remains were subsequently placed in a coffin and removed to Islington mortuary in Holloway Road.

The remains were examined by Dr Pepper, Master of Surgery of London University and a Fellow of the Royal College of Surgeons; Dr Herbert Willcox, senior analyst of the Home Office; and Dr Bernard Spilsbury (later Sir Bernard), pathologist at St Mary's Hospital, Paddington. It was to be the Crippen case that brought Spilsbury to public prominence and he was later a noted witness at several famous murder trials. The discovery of hyoscine hydrobromide led the pathologists to conclude that poisoning by the same was the cause of death. Hyoscine was sometimes used in a mild form in injections, but taken orally it caused certain death. A quarter of a grain to half a grain of hyoscine constitutes a fatal dose and the traces found in the remains amounted to two-fifths of a grain, which, according to the expert evidence given at Crippen's trial, corresponded to more than half a grain in the whole body. Pepper and Spilsbury concluded that the remains were those of a stout female who bleached her hair. Part of the flesh from the abdomen showed a scar, consistent with the ovariectomy undergone by Cora Crippen. Dr Willcox confirmed the presence of hyoscine, corroborating the evidence of Pepper and Spilsbury at the trial.

How did Crippen dispose of his wife's head, limbs and torso bones? There is a commonly held belief that her head was thrown overboard in a large handbag, carpetbag or hatbox, during the trip he took to Dieppe with Ethel Le Neve. Perhaps as a subtle act of

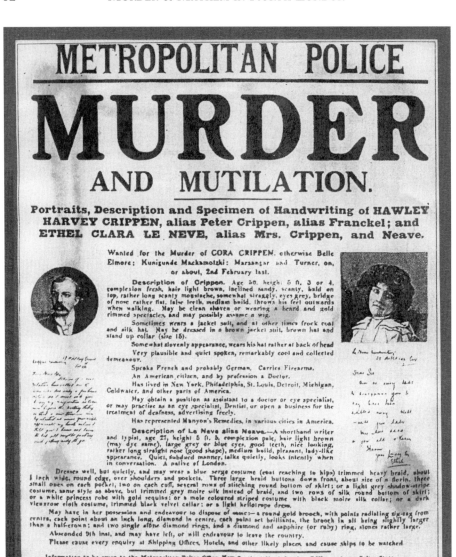

The Metropolitan Police wanted poster. Author's collection

vengeance, he burned as much as he could in the fire grate he had been forced to clean by his domineering wife. This particular method has been cited in several examinations of the case as the means of disposal, but it seems unlikely. The burning of flesh and bones in such large quantities would have created an awful stink in the street outside and for prolonged periods. Too much attention would have been drawn to the house if such a method had been used.

On 16 July, a warrant was issued for the arrest of both Crippen and Le Neve for murder and mutilation. The story made headline news and newpapers on both sides of the Atlantic and across Europe gave details of the gruesome discovery at Hilldrop Crescent and the search for the little doctor and his diminutive mistress. An official police description of Crippen read:

> Hawley Harvey Crippen: Age 50, 5ft. 3″ or 4″, complexion fresh, hair light brown, inclined sandy, scanty, bald on top, rather long scanty moustache, somewhat straggly, eyes grey, bridge of nose rather flat, false teeth, medium build, throws his feet outwards when walking ... Somewhat slovenly appearance, wears his hat rather at back of head. Very plausible and quiet spoken, remarkably cool and collected demeanour.

While Detective Chief Inspector Dew and Detective Sergeant Mitchell were making their discovery in the coal cellar at Hilldrop Crescent, the pair of lovers had fled the country to Belgium, and were staying at the *Hotel des Ardennes* in Brussels. In those days it was much easier to flee to the continent or indeed further afield, undetected, as passports were not required for travel. It was even possible to give a false name. Crippen, in his eagerness to flee London went a step further. He shaved off his moustache and removed his metal-framed spectacles. He also disguised Ethel as a boy, purporting to be his son. On Wednesday 20 July, having boarded the SS *Montrose* at Antwerp, as Mr John Philo Robinson and Master John Robinson, they set sail for Quebec, completely unaware that the hunt was already on for them.

Crippen's affection for Ethel Le Neve was to bring about his downfall. Despite the alteration to his appearance, he did not employ the same degree of care to changing his behaviour. Mr Robinson simply could not refrain from being over-affectionate to his sixteen-year-old son, with whom he shared Cabin 5. This odd behaviour between father and son soon captured the attention of the eagle-eyed Captain Kendall, who evidently fancied himself as an amateur sleuth, and he began to watch the couple's movements closely.

Captain Kendall had been given a description of Crippen and Le Neve at Millwall Docks on 14 July. Moreover, he bought a copy of the continental edition of the *Daily Mail* on 20 July and it contained pictures of the fugitives. Kendall noticed that although Mr Robinson did not wear spectacles, red marks on his nose suggested that he had done so until recently. Mr Robinson's displays of affection towards his son soon convinced the captain that master John Robinson was a woman. It did not take the captain long to put two and two together, and, having carefully studied Crippen's photograph, and, having allowed for the lack of moustaches and spectacles, he was soon convinced he had Crippen and Le Neve on board his ship. The captain did not waste any time in making use of the latest technological advancement which had only recently become available to him. He communicated his suspicions to Scotland Yard via the new Marconi Electric Telegraph. The SS *Montrose* was then only one of sixty ships in the world equipped with this device and this was the first time telegraph had ever been used to catch a criminal. The message conveyed the following information:

> Have reason to believe Dr Crippen and Miss Le Neve are travelling as passengers on my ship. They are posing as father and son and should reach Quebec on July 31. Await instructions. Kendall.

As soon as the News reached Scotland Yard, Detective Chief Inspector Dew made arrangements to travel to Quebec by a faster ship, the SS *Laurentic*, which set sail from Liverpool on 23 July and arrived in Quebec ahead of the SS *Montrose*.

While Dew was crossing the Atlantic, investigations continued in London. During routine enquiries in the vicinity of Hilldrop Crescent on 27 July a statement was taken from Lena Lyons by Sergeant C Cruchett, which took the following form:

> Statement made by Mrs Lena Lyons of 46 Brecknock Road, N., who says:
>
> > Between seven and eight o'clock one morning in either the latter end of January or the beginning of February last, whilst in bed I distinctly heard the sound of two shots. There was an interval of several seconds between each one. It was quite dark at the time and the sound startled me: they came from the direction of 39 Hilldrop Crescent. My lodger who at that time

occupied the first floor and slept in the back room overlooking 39 Hilldrop Crescent, came running down to my room. She said, 'Did you hear that shot Mrs Lyons?' I said 'Yes', and immediately we heard the second report.

I spoke to Mrs Lowe, the person next door, about it, also to my husband. He said it must have been a motor but I was convinced it was the sound of revolver shots. I only mention [sic] it to my husband and Mrs Lowe as people have spoken of Mrs Glackner of the Oil shop, 30 Brecknock Road, who said she heard screams, as an old gossip.

This statement was corroborated later that day in an account given by May Pole, Mrs Lyon's lodger.

Meanwhile, on board the SS *Montrose*, Dr Crippen and Ethel Le Neve, were throughout the entire eleven hour voyage blissfully unaware that their deception had been detected. Despite the unbridled hours of passion they were able to indulge themselves with in the privacy of their cabin, the little doctor's lack of restraint whilst in public areas gave rise to several wry smiles from the ship's officers who were in the know. Captain Kendall made full use of the Marconi Electric Telegraph by sending regular reports of the couple's activities. Every morning the *Daily Mail* reported the latest news on the fugitives and their pursuers.

On Sunday 31 July, the SS *Montrose* steamed slowly up the St Lawrence River towards Quebec. Mr Robinson was on deck, 'Master Robinson' was reading in Cabin 5. As Mr Robinson was taking in the sights, he noticed a pilot boat approaching, It came alongside and several people boarded the *Montrose*. The party included Detective Chief Inspector Dew, Detective Sergeant Mitchell and some female wardresses. Immediately on arrival on board Dew went to the bridge to pay his compliments to Captain Kendall. Formalities over, the small party made its way along the deck towards Mr Robinson. As the party drew near, Dew stepped forward and said:

Good morning Dr Crippen. I am Chief Inspector Dew of Scotland Yard. You will be arrested.

Crippen was startled at first. He had not recognised Dew immediately because without spectacles his vision was not particularly keen. Dew originally reported in 1910 that Ethel became 'agitated and fainted'. However, in his autobiography he said: 'With a shriek she collapsed.' Ethel's own account says:

> I remember that fateful Sunday morning that Dr Crippen pressed me after breakfast to go on deck with him. 'I don't think I will,' I said, 'It's very wretched up there, and I would rather stay down here and finish this book before lunch.' He went away quietly. Little did I know that I should not speak to him again for many days. A little time passed, and then the blow fell. There was a tap at the cabin door. I turned round quite naturally, expecting to see the doctor again. Instead I saw Inspector Dew! Even in his pilot's garb I did not fail to recognise him instantly.
>
> The sight of him stunned me. At this moment, for the first time, I realised there was something dreadful amiss. That this inspector should have chased us all the way from England filled me with horrible forebodings. I gave a cry, and then fell into a swoon.
>
> When I recovered I heard Inspector Dew read out his warrant for my arrest. I heard something about the 'murder and mutilation' of Mrs Crippen as in a dream. What it meant I did not know. Lately I had been thinking of Belle Elmore was alive, after all, and I had resolved when we reached Canada to confront the person who had sent the cablegrams to Dr Crippen. Now I was given to understand that not only was she dead, but murdered! Not only murdered, but that I was charged with being a party to the crime – a crime about which I knew absolutely nothing.

Following his arrest, two cards were found on Crippen. Both had the name John Robinson printed on them and were inscribed in pencil. The first read:

> I cannot stand the horror I go through every night any longer and as I see nothing ahead and money has come to an end, I have made up my mind to jump overboard tonight. I know I have spoiled your life but I'll hope some day you can learn to forgive me. Last words of love.
>
> Yours H

The second card read:

> Shall we wait till tonight about 10 or 11? If not, what time?

Some details concerning these cards came out at the trial when Crippen said that a quartermaster had brought him a letter explaining that Captain Kendall knew his and Miss Le Neve's true identities and they were to be arrested on arrival in Montreal. The quartermaster agreed to hide Crippen and help fake a suicide. He would go to Captain Kendall in the night and tell him he had heard a splash. On finding the cards, it would be assumed that Crippen had committed suicide. However, the arresting officers boarded the SS *Montrose* before the fake suicide plan could be implemented, and once the cards had been found, Crippen was shackled for his own protection.

After being detained in Canada for almost three weeks, Dr Crippen and Ethel Le Neve were brought back to England under arrest aboard the SS *Megantic*. Detective Inspector Dew travelled as Mr Doyle and Dr Crippen as Mr Nield. Crippen had already begun to grow his characteristic moustache again. Ethel was looked after by wardresses. The couple were not allowed to communicate. The next time they saw each other was in the dock at Bow Street magistrates' court. In *Ethel Le Neve: Her Life Story*, she recalled:

> The two wardresses who had been sent out to guard me never relaxed their vigilance. At night one of them always sat up with me while the other slept.
>
> Even now I think of one or two amusing incidents which relieved the monotony. Inspector Dew, who was always very kind, used to visit us often, and he was so paternal in his manner that we got accustomed to calling him 'Father.' 'Dear me, "father" is very grand to-night' we used to say when the inspector put on his evening dress and dined with the general company in the state saloon.
>
> When nearing Ireland we encountered very rough weather, and we all felt the effects of it. Inspector Dew himself fell victim to sea-sickness. On the landing-stage at Liverpool there was so great a crowd that I was nearly lost! The Canadian soldiers who had travelled over with us kept the throng back when it threatened to separate me and the two wardresses from the detectives who were in front in charge of Dr Crippen.
>
> It was only as I entered the train that I caught a glimpse of the doctor, huddled up between his guards. He looked very wistful, and saddened me. I nodded to him and smiled, just to cheer him

up, and his face brightened very much. At Euston there was another very large crowd to witness our arrival. But here, I am glad to say, I was allowed to walk across the platform just like an ordinary passenger to the taxi-cab which was waiting to convey me to the street.

When we reached the police-station we were taken at once into the charge-room. There Dr Crippen and I stood side by side while the same dreadful words about 'murder and mutilation' were read out. The next time I saw the doctor was when we passed into the dock at the police-court to begin the terrible ordeal of a public trial. Even in those painful surroundings it was a comfort to me to be near him again. Now and then we whispered together; but unfortunately, Dr Crippen is a little deaf in the left ear, and that was nearest to me, so that we could only have a few snatches of conversation.

At the police-court during the week which followed I heard the full details of the discovery at Hilldrop Crescent. All the time the evidence seemed to me utterly unreal and past belief. I could not associate the doctor with cruelty or crime. I knew him only as a man of tenderness and gentle nature, and it is thus that I now think of him.

It was thus that I thought of him when I sat in my lonely cell at the Old Bailey waiting wearily day after day while his trial was going on in the court above. They Allowed me to read the papers, and into my brain they burnt these dreadful things brought against him by the Crown.

The human remains found in the coal cellar at 39 Hilldrop Crescent, Lower Holloway, believed to be all that was salvageable of Cora Crippen, alias Belle Elmore, were interred at Finchley Cemetery on 10 October 1910. The cortege, consisting of a hearse and three mourning coaches, left Leverton's undertakers at 163 York Road, Camden Road, at 3.15pm. A few bits of flesh were retained as evidence.

Dr Crippen's trial began on Tuesday 18 October 1910 at the Old Bailey before the Lord Chief Justice Lord Alverstone, and lasted for five days. Ethel Le Neve did not appear in the dock with him. She would be tried separately with being an accessory after the fact. She did not give evidence at her lover's trial because Crippen insisted to his legal advisers that she should not be called as a witness on his behalf. Richard Muir appeared for the Crown and Crippen's defence was conducted by A A Tobin.

Mr Tobin contended that there was no proof that the remains found in the coal celler were those of a woman, let alone those of Dr Crippen's wife. Moreover, it was suggested that the remains had been buried in the cellar at 39 Hilldrop Crescent sometime before September 1905, when the Crippens had moved into the house. However, the tell-tale label on the pyjama jacket, bearing the words 'Shirtmakers

Hawley Harvey Crippen in the dock at the Old Bailey. Author's collection

Jones Brothers (Holloway) Limited, Holloway' proved beyond any reasonable doubt that the remains could have been buried in the cellar after the Crippens had moved in. When asked when he had purchased the pyjamas, Dr Crippen said they had been purchased in either 1905 or 1906. Crucially for the prosecution it emerged that Jones Brothers did not become a Limited Company until 1906 and labels did not include this until after that date. In addition the cloth from which the pyjama jacket was made 'did not come into existence' until November 1908, and it was proven that both the patterned cloth and the pyjamas were manufactured that same month. Never was circumstantial evidence so purely circumstantial and yet so damning.

During Mr Muir's final address he said:

There are two ways of approaching a question of identity. Find something which shows me that the remains here are the remains of Belle Elmore, that is one way; the other way is to see if there is something in these remains which shows that they are not the remains of Belle Elmore. My learned friend does not point to any single item in all the items in that grave for the purpose of saying there is a thing which shows that those remains cannot be the remains of Belle Elmore – not one. The only thing you find in the grave suggestive of a man are suggestive of the man who put them there. No medical man can say with certainty on anatomical grounds that those remains are the remains of a woman. Further, anatomical grounds are the only grounds upon which as medical men, they would be justified in forming any medical opinion at all. But what follows? Hinde's curlers with human hair – a woman's hair – were mixed up with those remains. How did they get there unless they came from the body of which those remains are all that are left? The colour of the hair is dark brown, bleached to a lighter colour. Belle Elmore had dark brown hair bleached to a lighter colour. True, other women undoubtedly have dark brown hair bleached to a lighter colour, but there is no suggestion that any woman with hair of that sort has been missing in London within the limits of time which are involved in this case. Mrs Harrison, one of Belle Elmore's oldest friends in this country, has often seen her dressing, and speaks to the hair being like the hair of Belle Elmore as she saw it before it was bleached. Mrs Harrison speaks of the undergarments as being such as Belle Elmore always wore.

Mr Muir then went on to commend the jury for their bravery in examining the flesh produced in evidence and then went on to discuss the defence's assertion that the medical evidence with regard to a piece of flesh supposedly from the abdominal wall, would leave the jury in such doubt as to acquit Crippen, then added:

Dr Pepper, a surgeon of the greatest experience, who in practice in London has himself performed hundreds of operations and has seen the scars, after they have healed, which have been caused by his own operations, says they were just such scars as this – wide at the bottom, narrowing towards the top. Dr Pepper said, 'I have seen that in many cases of operations which I have performed myself.' Dr Willcox, a surgeon of great experience, and Dr Maxwell, the police surgeon, also saw this flesh before it had been preserved. All of them saw it. All of them say it is a scar … Dr Turnbull has examined it microscopically, so has Dr Spilsbury …

Mr Muir then turned to doubt cast on the piece of flesh that contained the mark, testified by the various medical men to being a scar:

It was suggested that this was not a scar at all, that it was caused by a fold; and you have the advantage of having the specimen,

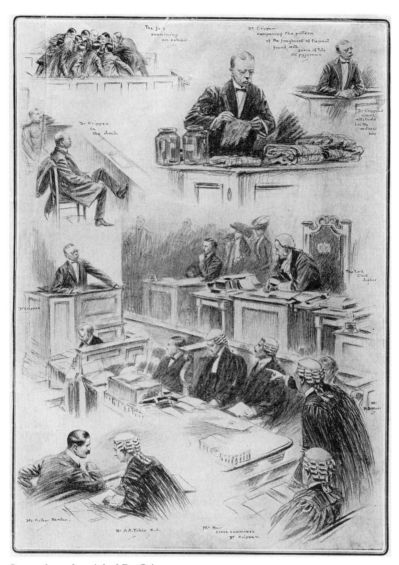

Scenes from the trial of Dr Crippen. Author's collection

and the surgeon before you, and seeing and judging for yourselves the weight and the authority of the evidence upon that point ... Is that a piece of the lower abdominal wall of a human being? As to his [Dr Crippen's] anatomy, or his lack of it, you will have to decide upon the evidence which has been given. His diploma of anatomy, or surgery, showed that he passed or satisfied the authorities at the college he attended upon the subject. His own statement says he attended hospitals in London, before taking his degree, with a purpose of witnessing operations. This is not a delicate task which requires constant skill and practice – constant practice in order to do it with accuracy – but it does require medical knowledge; it does require some degree of dexterity. Such, says Dr Pepper, would be acquired by going through the medical school, and would not be lost by ten years of want of practice. Somebody in Crippen's house, while Crippen was the tenant of it, carved up that body, which I suggest to you upon the evidence is proved to be the body of Cora Crippen, the wife of the prisoner. Who could have done this thing in Crippen's house since November 1908? The man who is now on his trial ... Is that fact explicable on any hypothesis except one, and that hypothesis that Crippen knew when those remains were buried in the cellar, and that any inquiry to find her would be undoubtedly fruitless ... The newspapers of two continents are ringing with this case. The police are inquiring and circulating the descriptions, and it is solemnly suggested to you that Belle Elmore might be alive! Is it not asking you to behave like children in a nursery listening to fairy-tales, to act on such a suggestion as that? You are grown men, business men. If ever a fact were proved beyond a doubt, beyond a reasonable doubt to business men, courageously applying their minds to a difficult and painful task, has not this fact been proved beyond all reasonable doubt – that Belle Elmore is dead? How did she die? She died of hyoscine poisoning, and the poison hyoscine was found in those remains – the remains of Belle Elmore. How did it come there? Crippen bought hyoscine on January 19, five grains of it. He had never bought it before, never bought it since. What did he do with it? Two and a third grains he said he dispensed in those medicines used in extraordinarily rare and difficult cases. Not the kind of cases ordinarily dealt with through the post. No patient called who ever got a pilule with hyoscine in it.

During his summing up, after reminding the jury that the prisoner must have the benefit of any reasonable doubt, Lord Alverstone continued:

You must not allow doubt as to whether minor points have been established to influence you, if upon the whole of the evidence you have no doubt. Mr Tobin in his speeches to you, used, two or three times, the expression 'certainty'. Rightly understood, that is not a misleading word, but if by that it is to be supposed that jurors are not to act upon evidence that puts them in the position of having actually seen a thing done, it is, of course, a misleading expression ... In this case Crippen is said to have wilfully and intentionally poisoned his wife, mutilated the body, and buried the remains in the cellar at Hilldrop Crescent, in order to conceal his crime ... There is no suggestion that by some other means or method or agency Dr Crippen caused the death of his wife. The first question is: Were the remains found at 39 Hilldrop Crescent those of Cora Crippen? If they were not, there is an end of the case. If you find that they were the remains of Cora Crippen, then you have to ask yourselves: 'Was her death occasioned by the wilful act of the defendant, Crippen? ... 'No,' he says, 'I will tell you what has happened to the woman as far as I know; she is not dead to my knowledge; she left me of her own accord, some time after one and two or two and three o'clock on the morning of February 1, and six and seven o'clock in the evening when I returned to my house.' That is the defence put forward by Crippen, which you must carefully consider. If made out you need not trouble any more about whose the remains were. If the body in the cellar was not the body of Cora Crippen, the defendant is entitled to go out of this court. Whatever may be your ultimate view in this case, you will agree that the defendant is an extraordinary man. If he is guilty, as you might think, he is still more an extraordinary man – he has committed a callous crime; he has covered up that callous crime – has endeavoured to cover it, in a callous way; and he has behaved with the most brutal callousness and indifference after the crime was committed. If he is an innocent man it is almost impossible to fathom his mind and his character – absolutely indifferent to charges made against him of murder; having the means of doing his utmost to establish his innocence, yet taking no step of any sort or kind, although defended by an able solicitor, and though he could fairly and properly have any step taken, so far as the evidence before you is concerned, to support and establish by other evidence the statement which he made in the box ... It is most material to examine with some little care whether the arguments of Mr Muir or the arguments of Mr Tobin are well founded. Mr Tobin says that Belle Elmore may be alive. He says that sometimes people have been convicted when the supposed murdered person is walking about the world. 'This may be one of those cases; be careful how you act.' That is a perfectly proper caution ... You cannot rely on the mere statements made by Dr Crippen. He has on his own confession lied for his own purpose and for the purpose of his own advantage. Even when he was purporting to tell the truth certain things were false and false to his own knowledge. Here again, let me caution you. This is not a court of morals, but a court of law. The fact that Belle Elmore was an immoral woman at some time or another, that the man confessed to having been an immoral man, and having been living in improper circumstances with Ethel Le Neve, is a matter you may regret in your own minds, but all that you are entitled to do is to take into consideration those circumstances as far as they have a direct bearing on the case. The fact that Dr Crippen has lied on material points in this case is a very important matter for your consideration. I will tell you why. It is said by the Crown that Crippen's conduct Crippen's lies, Crippen's life from February 1 until the end of July was impossible if there was any risk of his wife reappearing. What Mr Muir put to him, and has impressed upon you, is that the story that his wife left him on February 1 cannot be true, because of the things which Crippen did from February down to July ... Mr Muir says that the life of this man was an utter impossibility unless he knew his wife would never return again. What was the character of the woman? Her character and habits are not disputed. She was a woman who had had a past ... a woman making warm friendships, very bright, very vivacious. They had a position of very considerable comfort, having, according to Crippen, plenty of money, having a most remarkable amount of valuable jewellery, and therefore the woman as many women in that class of life are, very fond of wearing it, and very fond of fine clothes. Therefore she is in a position that many women of the walk in life would aspire to. The wife of a man, reputable in the public eye, living comfortably and happily in Hilldrop Crescent for more than four years before she disappears. There is nothing strange about the fact that there is no servant kept. Many people of that class adopt a similar method, just having a charwoman to do the odd work ... She is obviously a popular woman ... It is a very serious suggestion made to you by counsel for the defence that Belle Elmore may be alive. If Belle Elmore is alive is it possible to think that this has come to her knowledge, and that she is so mean and abominably wicked as to allow this man to stand for trial in the dock? I assume now you will approach the matter with a view to considering whether the Crown have made out their case, and not whether the prisoner's story was correct.

On the fifth day of the trial, having heard all the evidence, the jury retired and returned after only twenty-seven minutes with a guilty verdict. Sentence of death was pronounced.

In her own account, Ethel described her feelings after her lover's trial came to its conclusion:

> When his ordeal was over they drove me away in complete ignorance of his fate. I was yearning to know the verdict, but it was kept from me. It was two days afterwards when the Governor of Holloway Prison broke the news to me.

Ethel Le Neve's trial began on 25 October and lasted just one day. She appeared before the same judge and the same prosecutor as Dr Crippen. She was defended by E E Smith KC, afterwards the First Earl of Birkenhead. She gave no evidence, but was acquitted and set free.

Dr Crippen's appeal, having been was heard, failed on 5 November, his execution took place on the morning of 23 November 1910. Crippen's executioner was John Ellis, who was a barber and publican when not engaged on 'government work'. He was held in high regard for his efficiency. After Ellis removed the doctor's spectacles, Crippen made a last request to the prison governor, Major Owen Edward Mytton-Davies, that a photograph of Ethel and her letters be buried with him. He went to his death calmly. At the time of Crippen's execution three other men were awaiting execution at Pentonville Prison. On the occasion of Crippen's execution the traditional tolling of the prison bell to signify that an execution had taken place was dispenses with. This was in consideration of the three other condemned men's feelings. The bell was never again tolled to mark an execution. Shortly after Crippen had been hanged, two notices were posted on the prison gates. The first notice was the 'Declaration of the Sheriff and Others,' confirming that judgement of death had been carried out; and the second was the 'Cerificate of the Surgeon' which confirmed that the prisoner Crippen was dead.

Once Crippen had been pronounced dead, his body was left hanging on the locked execution shed for the customary one hour.

Afterwards the body was stripped by the executioner and his assistant and taken to the mortuary for a post-mortem examination and inquest. Later that morning, at around noon, Crippen's body was buried in the prison yard under 8 feet of earth, along with a photograph of Ethel Le Neve.

As for Ethel Le Neve, within three hours of the little doctor's execution, she set sail aboard the SS *Majestic* bound for New York. Dressed in mourning, a veil hiding her face, she was entered on the passenger list as 'Miss Allen'. Ethel stayed briefly in New York before travelling on to Canada, where she settled in Toronto and worked as a typist. Early in 1911, she was granted probate of Crippen's will, valued at £268. Letters of administration regarding Mrs Crippen's estate were granted to Mrs Theresa Hunn (Cora Crippen's sister, Tessie). Ethel could not settle comfortably in Canada without the little doctor by her side and she returned to England in 1914. Once again Ethel settled in London and found employment as a typist at Hampton's furniture store in Trafalgar Square, where she worked under the surname of Harvey, her late lover's middle name.

It was while she was working at Hampton's that Ethel met her husband to be, accountant Stanley Smith, from Croydon, who also worked there. They married and had a son and daughter. In *The Crippen Files*, compiled by Jonathan Goodman, there is a faded photograph of Stanley Smith. He had a moustache not unlike Crippen's, and although he had more hair and his eyes were not quite so bulging, his physical resemblance to the little doctor is remarkable. Stanley Smith suffered a heart attack at work shortly before his seventieth birthday when he was due to retire. He was, apparently, completely unaware of his wife's true identity.

Ursula Bloom, the famous journalist, discovered Ethel's whereabouts in 1954 and interviewed her. Faithful to the end, Ethel maintained that the little doctor knew nothing about the remains found at Hilldrop Crescent and was innocent of any crime. Ethel lived out the remainder of her life between London and 10 Parkway Road, Addiscombe, in relative obscurity. She died a widow, aged eighty-four, in Dulwich Hospital, on 9 August 1967. She requested that a gilt locket containing a picture of Dr Crippen which she had held on to through the long years since 1910, should be placed in her coffin.

As for other people connected with the Crippen case, Crippen's solicitor Arthur Newton had been allowed access to Crippen while he was under sentence of death. Following the execution, for financial gain, Newton colluded with various newspapers and journals regarding a letter supposedly written by Crippen after the trial, in which he confessed to the murder and mutilation of his wife. Newton knew that this claim was completely untrue. No such letter existed. As a result of his professional misconduct the King's Bench Division of the High Court suspended him for twelve months, from 12 July 1911. In 1913, Newton was sentenced to three years' penal servitude for defrauding an Austrian business-man. On his release from Parkhurst, he was struck from the rolls by the Law Society. He became a private investigator and died in 1930.

Captain Henry Kendall was involved in a near fatal accident four years after the Crippen case, when in 1914, the ship he com-manded, the *Empress of Ireland,* sank off Father Point, Quebec, near the spot where the little doctor and Ethel were arrested. That same year the SS *Montrose* sank close to Dover's famous white cliffs.

Chief Inspector Walter Dew retired at forty-seven years old, just three weeks before Crippen was hanged. This early retirement was allegedly brought about because of the sympathy he felt for Crippen. His memoirs, *I Caught Crippen,* were published in 1938. Walter Dew died in Worthing, in 1947.

John Ellis, Crippen's executioner, resigned in 1924. In the course of twenty-three years he had executed 203 men and women. Later that year Ellis tried to commit suicide. After drink-ing heavily, he attempted to shoot himself through the head. He bungled it and succeeded only in fracturing his jaw. He appeared before a magistrate who told him:

> I am sorry to see you here Ellis. I have known you for a long time. If your aim was as true as some of the drops you have given, it would have been a bad job for you.

Ellis was bound over to keep the peace for a year and to stay away from strong drinks and thoughts of suicide. He became very depressed. His health was not good and he continued to drink heavily. In September 1932, nine years after he had first attempted suicide, he slit his throat with a cut-throat razor. This time he did not bungle it. He was fifty-eight years of age. The coroner's verdict was 'Suicide while of unsound mind'.

CHAPTER 5

Murder by Arsenic Poisoning – or did an Innocent Man Hang?
Finsbury Park, 1912

... she said that Lloyd George's budget had upset licensed premises by increased taxation.

rederick Seddon was born in Lancashire at the height of Queen Victoria's reign. By the Edwardian period he was working in London, employed as District Superintendent of Canvassers for North London with the Manchester Industrial Assurance Company, a position he had occupied since 1901. He was a freemason and one-time chapel-goer and preacher. He had a fascination with money and all things financial from an early age. He fully appreciated the value of money and was hard working, thrifty and eager to save. In his quest to make money he was willing to turn his hand to any type of business and took pride in attending to even the simplest of transactions in meticulous detail. This overtly precise man had one major failing: he was not particularly likeable, although clearly likeable enough to enable him to obtain a wife. His general manner and air of superiority tended to alienate him from those he came into contact with. His lack of affability went strongly against him and formed a major part in his downfall when he went on trial for his life, accused of murder.

Seddon's lack of affability is evident in the trial transcript. That he was guilty of the crime of which he was convicted and hanged is open to considerable doubt and, despite there being an enormous public outcry at his trial's verdict; and a petition bearing more than 250,000 signatures claiming his innocence, his execution was still allowed to go ahead. Many criminologists and commentators insist that Seddon was indeed innocent of the murder of Miss Eliza

Barrow; and having sifted through many documents associated with the Seddon case I am inclined to take that view myself.

In 1909, when this particular account begins, in addition to his insurance work, Seddon owned a second-hand clothes business which he ran in his wife's name, at 276 Seven Sister's Road, Finsbury Park, and he and his family lived above the shop. Seddon invested his additional income in mortgaged property and regularly sold it on for profit. After one successful business deal, he bought a fourteen-room house at 63 Tollington Park, situated north of Seven Sisters Road between Stroud Green Road and Hornsey Road, in the area of North London that lies between Holloway and Finsbury Park. The house was originally purchased as an investment to turn into flats, but Seddon was quick to realise that this particular house could provide a home for himself and his family, as well as a basement office; and there would still be room for tenants in the four rooms on the top floor.

In November 1909, the family moved in. Seddon's insurance company employers found him scrupulously honest and so exact in his accounting that they allowed him to bank their money in his own account, and were pleased to give him 5*s* a week rent for his basement room office in which he administered their business. For the convenience of business callers to the house, the basement could be reached by an outside flight of steps. An inside flight led to the other parts of the building.

Towards the end of the year Mr and Mrs Seddon fell out and briefly separated, but their differences were soon mended and Margaret Seddon found herself pregnant again with her fifth child. Then, on 20 June 1910, Seddon instructed a local house agent to obtain a tenant for his top floor, for which he would receive a rental income of 12*s* 6*d* a week. The two other floors and the basement were occupied by the Seddon household – Mrs and Mrs Seddon, Mr Seddon's seventy-three-year-old father, William Seddon, four children (with a fifth to follow) and an eccentric servant named Mary Chater, a former mental nurse who was somewhat unhinged herself. The Seddons also employed a charwoman, Mrs Rutt, although she lived elsewhere. As well as the rental income he received from his company and for the top floor, Seddon also charged his two sons 6*s* a week for living at home.

Behind its yellow and red brick façade, 63 Tollington Park was a substantial house. In the basement, as well as the office there was a back kitchen. There were two reception rooms on the raised

No 63 Tollington Park. Paul T Langley Welch

ground floor. On the first floor the two bedrooms had been divided by means of partitions to provide space for all the Seddon family, which including the servant, Mary Chater, the household comprising nine people. As well as Frederick and Margaret Seddon and Seddon's father, there was seventeen-year-old William, Maggie, aged sixteen, Freddie, aged fifteen, Ada, aged eight and Lily, who was at that time not yet one.

Eliza Barrow was a forty-nine-year-old spinster of independent means, with private property amounting to about £4,000, which included the *Buck's Head* and adjacent barber's shop in Camden Town. She had taken on the responsibility for two orphaned children of a former landlady in Clapton. An adolescent girl called Hilda was away at boarding school, but eight-year-old Ernie Grant lived with Miss Barrow in a succession of lodgings. In about May 1909, they went to lodge with Miss Barrow's cousins, Mr and Mrs Frank Vonderahe, at 31 Evershot Road, a turning off Tollington Park. However, Frank and Julia Vonderahe and Miss Barrow did not get on and Miss Barrow once spat at Mrs Vonderahe. Miss Barrow decided to look for lodgings with her friend Mr and Mr Robert Hook and move out of her cousin's house; and they all moved into 63 Tollington Park. Mr Hook was an engine-driver and he and his wife were to lodge with Miss Barrow in exchange for Mrs Hook's domestic services.

By 1 August 1910, thirteen people were living in Seddon's house. It was not long before Miss Barrow found fault with the Hooks. Miss Barrow was not a very likeable person and most people found her difficult to get on with, as became clear during the evidence given by various witnesses at the Seddon's trial. Seddon became aware of the lack of harmony on the top floor and decided that Miss Barrow and the Hooks were not suitable tenants. He informed Miss Barrow that they would have to leave. However, when Miss Barrow turned to Seddon for help with her financial matters, she convinced him that it was the Hooks who were at fault. He was persuaded to allow Miss Barrow and little Ernie to remain on the top floor of his house and only the Hooks were asked to leave. They did so very quickly after Seddon posted a notice to quit on their door.

Frederick Seddon found a soulmate in Miss Barrow. Like him, Eliza Barrow had a fondness for money and investments. She stood about 5 feet 4 inches tall and was rather plump. During the trial, evidence was given that she dressed badly, was parsimonious

in her habits and had been prone to alcoholic indulgence. She paid
12s 6d in rent for her rooms, and, following the departure of the
Hooks, 7s a week to the Seddon's daughter Maggie, for cooking
and cleaning.

Following Lloyd George's budget in 1909, like many other
ladies of her class in similar circumstances, Miss Barrow had
become increasingly concerned that his 'soak the rich' policy
would reduce her to penury. At the trial Seddon said of her:

> It was her property that was worrying her. She said she had a
> public house in Camden Town called the *Buck's Head*, and it was
> the principal source of her income; she had a lot of trouble with
> the ground landlords, and she said that Lloyd George's Budget
> had upset licensed premises by increased taxation.

Seddon gave Miss Barrow reassurance and offered her financial
advice. This culminated in their coming to a financial arrangement
that would benefit both parties. In exchange for an annuity,
amounting to £52, Seddon took from Miss Barrow a seventeen-
year lease on the *Buck's Head* and the adjacent 1 Buck Street, a
small building then occupied by a barber's shop. On 14 October
1910, Miss Barrow transferred ownership of her India Stock,
valued at £1,600, to Seddon. He agreed to pay her a lifetime
annuity, amounting to £103 4s, in addition to the £52 to which he
had already committed. Seddon sold the India Stock for £1,520
and invested the money in fourteen tenement houses in London's
East End, at Coutts Road, Stepney, for a rental income of £200 a
year. Seddon paid Miss Barrow her annuity in regular instalments
and she was delighted, because the money she received as a result
of Seddon's financial advice exceeded the amount she had been
receiving in dividends.

London sweltered in a heatwave during the last week of August
and the first week of September 1911. On the morning of Friday
1 September, Miss Barrow was taken ill with what was diagnosed
by Dr Sworn as epidemic diarrhoea. He prescribed bismuth and
morphia. He said she was very ill and added that her mental
condition appeared as bad as her physical health. He returned on
the Saturday and on the Sunday, but there was no improvement.
Miss Bartrow found it difficult to take her medication, so he gave
her an effervescing mixture of citrate of potash and bicarbonate of
soda. He could give her nothing for the diarrhoea, which was very

severe. Dr Sworn stated at the trial, when asked if there was an epidemic of flies at the time:

> I have never seen so many as I saw in that room. I put it down to the smell of the motions which would attract them.

The doctor suggested that she should go to hospital, but Miss Barrow refused. She also refused to have a nurse, saying that Mrs Seddon could attend to her needs.

On Monday 4 September, Mrs Seddon said that Miss Barrow instructed her to go and get some flypapers. She did not want the sticky type but those that you wet. On Tuesday, Miss Barrow was a little better and she called for Ernie Grant to sleep with her, which was her habit (little Ernie referred to Miss Barrow as 'Chickie'). For the next three days Dr Sworn continued prescribing the effervescing medicine but on the 9th he gave Miss Barrow an additional blue pill containing mercury, as 'her motion was so offensive'. The stench emanating from Miss Barrow's room permeated the entire house. It became so bad that carbolic sheets were hung in the rooms in an attempt to fumigate the air.

Miss Barrow began to grow worried about what would happen to little Ernie and Hilda if she were to die. She asked Seddon to draw up a will for her. He did so and the will was witnessed by his married sister, Emily Longley, who was visiting at the time, and Mrs Seddon. The will made Frederick H Seddon sole executor, 'to hold all my personal belongings, furniture, clothing and jewellery in trust' until Ernest and Hilda Grant came of age. Miss Eliza Barrow died at about 6.15am on Thursday 14 September 1911. Seddon went to Dr Sworn's house and told him the news. The doctor made out a death certificate, giving the cause of death as 'epidemic diarrhoea'.

William Nodes, undertaker, operated from 201 Holloway Road and had a branch office at 78 Stroud Green Road, a short distance from Seddon's house. Seddon called on Mr Nodes at about 11.30am on 14 September, to arrange Miss Barrow's funeral. The funeral took place two days later. When giving evidence at the trial, Mr Nodes was asked questions regarding the funeral arrangements and what some might consider the unseemly haste in which Miss Barrow was buried. Mr Nodes stated:

> If we did not Bury on Saturday it would mean burying on Monday, and having regard to the state that the body was in and

the diarrhoea that had taken place, the warmth of the weather, and the fact that there was no lead lining to the coffin, it seemed quite reasonable that the body should be buried on Saturday . . . I explained to him what kind of funeral it would be for the price; it was a £4 funeral really, and it would mean a coffin, polished and ornamented with handles and inside lining, a composite carriage, the necessary bearers, and the fees to Islington Cemetery, and it included the internment in the grave at Finchley. I do not know that I specified what kind of grave she would be buried in, but it would mean internment in a public grave, a grave dug by the cemetery people, who allow internments in it at a certain price, which included the use of the clergyman. By a 'public grave' I mean a grave which is not the particular property of any individual; it is used for more than one person. I think it was distinctly understood by Mr Seddon that it would not be a private grave.

Seddon was quick to point out that Miss Barrow was not a relation of his and, in consideration of the business he had brought him, accepted 12s 6d commission from William Nodes. The funeral took place on Saturday afternoon; Mr and Mrs F H Seddon and William Seddon travelled in the composite carriage to the cemetery in East Finchley.

On 20 September, Frank Vonderahae heard that his cousin had been ill and called to see her. He was amazed when the Seddons' maid told him that she had died and that the funeral had already taken place. The Vonderahaes called again to see Mr Seddon, who told them he had written to them in Evershot Street, telling them about the death and showed them a copy of his letter. The Vonderahaes said they had moved to Corbyn Street, but letters were forwarded to them and they had never received it. Seddon's copy of the letter was later produced in evidence in court:

63 Tollington Park, London N
14th Septr., 1911.
Mr. Frank E. Vonderahe.

Dear Sir,
I sincerely regret to have to inform you of the death of your Cousin, Miss Eliza Mary Barrow, at 6.00am this morning, from epidemic diarrhoea. The funeral will take place on Saturday next about 1.00 to 2.00pm.

Please inform Albert, Edward and Emma Vonderahe of her decease, and let me know if you or they wish to attend the funeral.

I must also inform you that she made a 'will' on the 11th instant leaving what she died possessed of to Hilda and Ernest Grant, and appointed myself as sole executor under the 'will'.

Yours respectfully,

F. H. Seddon

Mr. Frank Ernest Vonderahe,

31, Evershot Road,

Finsbury Park, N.

The Vonderahes admitted that they had no particular liking for Miss Barrow, but they expressed astonishment that she had not been buried in the family vault in Highgate Cemetery. In it were buried Miss Barrow's parents and several close relatives and Miss Barrow had always believed that that would also be her final resting place. Seddon said that he believed that the vault was full, but the Vonderahes contradicted him. Seddon told them that it would be an easy matter if the family wished to have Miss Barrow's body moved to Highgate. The Vonderahes did not want to pursue the point, but they were anxious to know what had happened to Eliza Barrow's money. Robert Hook later testified that Miss Barrow had £420 4s 3d, mostly in gold coin, when he helped her to count it in 1906, and the money was kept in fifteen bags in a cash-box. The Vonderahes also knew that Miss Barrow had a considerable sum of cash. When Seddon told them there wasn't any, they weren't satisfied. They created a fuss and became highly suspicious about the circumstances surrounding their cousin's death. They continued to pester and accuse, and eventually decided to support their suspicions to the police, who began an investigation.

Miss Barrow's body was exhumed on 15 November and examined by pathologist Dr Bernard Spilsbury, in the presence of Dr William Willcox, at Finchley Mortuary. The body was in a remarkable state of preservation. Virtually no decomposition had taken place, although, as is usual, the body had lost a considerable amount of its water content. Traces of arsenic were found in her stomach as well as other parts of her organs; and in the extremities of her finger nails and her hair. An inquest was opened on 23 November at Friern Barnet, before the coroner for Central Middlesex, Dr George Cohen, at which both Mr and Mrs Seddon gave evidence. In his report to the coroner's court, Dr Spilsbury stated:

> I found no disease in any of the organs sufficient to account for death, except in the stomach and intestines. In the intestines I found a little reddening of the inner surface of the upper part . . . The body was remarkably well preserved, both externally and internally. This would suggest that death was due to some poison having a preservative effect, or to the presence of some preserving agent. I think the arsenic that Dr Willcox says he found would account for the preservation of the body . . . The reddening was evidence of inflammation. I don't think there is anything to distinguish this from natural gastro-enteritis.

Dr Willcox stated that in his opinion there must have been more than two grains of arsenic present in the body at the time of death; that the death was due to acute arsenical poisoning and that Miss Barrow must have taken a moderately large fatal dose, less than three, and probably less than two, days before her death. The inquest was adjourned for three weeks to enable further investigations to be made.

On 29 November, Dr Willcox made a further examination of Miss Barrow's remains and found arsenic present in all the organs and other parts tested. Neither the family nor the authorities transferred Miss Barrow's body to Highgate Cemetery, made possible by he exhumation. In due course it was returned to another grave in the cemetery at East Finchley.

On the evening of Monday 4 December, at 7.00pm, Frederick Seddon was arrested outside his home, just as he was about to take a walk. When he was just a few paces from his gateway, his progress was stopped by Chief Inspector Wood. According to the inspector, when he was told he would be arrested for the wilful murder of Miss Eliza Barrow and for administering poison, Seddon replied:

> Absurd. What a terrible charge – wilful murder. It is the first of [sic] our family that has ever been charged with such a crime. Are you going to arrest my wife as well? If not I would like you to give her a message from me. Have they found arsenic in her body? . . . It was not carbolic acid was it, as there was some of it in her room?

At the time of his arrest, as well as 63 Tollington Park, Seddon owned seventeen other properties, The inquest was resumed on

14 December. Frederick Seddon attended in custody and reserved his evidence for the trial that was to follow. The jury returned their verdict as follows:

> That the said Eliza Mary Barrow died on the 14th of September, 1911, of arsenical poisoning at 63, Tollington Park, the arsenic having been administered to her by some person or persons unknown. And so the jurors aforesaid do further say that the said person or persons unknown on the 13th or 14th or 13th and 14th days of September, 1911, did feloniously, wilfully, and of malice aforethought murder and slay against the peace of our Lord the King, his Crown and Dignity, the said Eliza Mary Barrow.

During the weeks that followed Eliza Barrow's death Mrs Seddon had exchanged thirty-three £5 notes in local shops. Their serial numbers showed them to have been Miss Barrow's. Mrs Seddon never gave a satisfactory explanation for having endorsed them as 'Mrs Scott' of 10 or 18 Evershot Street. In those days it was necessary to endorse high value banknotes when exchanging them in whole or in part for goods or services.

Mrs Margaret Seddon was arrested on 15 January 1912.

The trial of forty-year-old Frederick Henry Seddon and thirty-eight-year-old Margaret Anne Seddon opened on 4 March 1912 at the Central Criminal Court in the Sessions House, Old Bailey, before Mr Justice Bucknill and lasted for ten days. Counsel for the Crown was led by the Attorney-General, the Right Honourable Sir Rufus D Isaacs KC, MP, R D Muir, S A T Rowlatt and Travers Humphreys. Counsel for Frederick H Seddon were Edward Marshall Hall KC, MP, Mr Dunstan and Mr Orr; and For Margaret A Seddon, Gervais Rentoul.

The weight of evidence assembled against the Seddons centered on the amount of arsenic found in Miss Barrow's remains and the acquisition of flypapers containing arsenic. Flypapers had been purchased at Thorley's Chemists at 27 Crouch Hill. Walter Thorley knew the Seddons' daughter Margaret (Maggie) because she was friendly with his own daughter. Mr Thorley testified that:

> On 26th August, 1911, Margaret Seddon purchased from me a threepenny packet of Mather's fly-papers. There were six fly-papers now shown to me, exhibit 136. Outside that packet I see 'Mather's Chemical Fly-papers. To poison flies, wasps, ants, mosquitoes, &c. Prepared only by the sole proprietors,

W. Mather Limited, Dyer Street, Manchester. Poison. These arsenic fly-papers can only be sold by registered chemists, and in accordance with the provisions of the Pharmacy Act.' The words 'these arsenic fly-papers,' are in larger print than the other portion of the sentence. Taking one of the papers out, I find that in the centre it contains the following:- 'Directions for use. For flies, wasps, ants, mosquitoes etc., spread each paper on a dish or plate and keep moist with cold water. A little sugar, beer, or wine added two or three times a day makes them more attractive. Caution. Remove the tray or dish beyond the reach of children and out of the way of domestic animals.' Then at the bottom of it, there is 'Poison.' I would not like to say definitely how many grains of arsenic there are in each of these fly-papers; there might be more in one than in another. I do not keep any note of my sales. I think there is a large sale for those fly-papers; I myself sold many of them last year . . .

It was shown that, if boiled, one flypaper could produce 5 grains of arsenic, 2 grains being a fatal dose: 2.1 grains were found in Miss Barrow's remains. Various theories were put forward as to how arsenic might have got into Miss Barrow's body. It was suggested that she might have taken it herself in small quantities over a long period, a practice considered beneficial in some quarters. Mr Marshall Hall was not convinced that all the tests made on Miss Barrow's body gave an accurate reading of the amount of arsenic the body contained, due to the body having shrunk as a result of water loss. Regarding the famous Marsh test, conducted by Dr Willcox and used to establish the amount of arsenic contained in the body, Mr Marshall Hall said:

It is theory, that is all. It is scientific theory of the highest possible character, but he cannot prove it to me by ocular demonstration, and it is not the sort of theory upon which a man's life ought to be put in peril.

Regarding the 2.1 grains of arsenic found in Miss Barrow's body tissue, he said:

Dr Willcox admits that that is purely a matter of calculation. You cannot get at that for this reason, that you cannot get at the weight of the muscle tissue, and therefore you have to estimate it. It has never been estimated on a dead body, and therefore you have to deal with it with a live body, and with a live body it is calculated that the muscle tissue accounts for 44 per cent – three fifths [sic] of the total weight of the body; that is the total weight of the live body. This body had shrunk from something like 10 stones to under 5 stones, so that there was a wastage of half.

Mr Marshall Hall continued to protest that the calculation made concerning the quantity of arsenic in the body had not been accurately calculated and therefore did not present the true facts. He completed this point by adding:

> What I say is this, and what I ask you to find as a fact in this case is this, that there is arsenic in this body, that it did not cause the death, that she died of gastro-enteritis – that is, that is that she died of epidemic diarrhoea. Possibly the condition may have been aggravated, but that there is no evidence in the body was of itself sufficient to cause death, because you cannot rely scientifically on the quantity alleged to have been found.

Despite Mr Marshall Hall's magnificent defence, Frederick Seddon's own performance in the witness box went against him. He was simply not a likeable man. The often flippant or glib answers Seddon gave under cross-examination did not endear him to the jury. The Attorney-General, Sir Rufus D Isaacs, asked Seddon:

> Miss Barrow lived with you from 26th July 1910, till the morning of 14th September 1911?

Seddon replied:

> Yes.

Sir Rufus then asked:

> Did you like her?

Seddon replied with a question:

> Did I like her?

Sir Rufus then said:

> Yes, that is the question.

Seddon replied:

> She was not a woman that you could be in love with, but I deeply sympathised with her.

Scenes from the trial of the Seddons. Illustrated Police News.

Later, Sir Rufus said:

I should like you to understand, if the ordinary expectation of her life was twenty-one-years – the life of a woman of that age – and you thought, as you told us, it was going to be less than that, what sort of view did you form in your own mind about it?

Seddon replied:

I could not say; I could not tell how long the woman was going to live.

Sir Rufus asked:

But some years less?

To which Seddon replied:

I have known people in consumption outlive healthy people; as the old saying is, 'A creaky gate hangs a long time.'

Much of the evidence assembled against the Seddons was circumstantial. However, it was Mrs Seddon who had continuous access to the sickroom and it was she who is known to have endorsed £165 in £5 notes, using a false name following Miss Barrow's death (at today's values about £8,250). That Frederick Seddon had expressed his willingness to look after little Ernie following Miss Barrow's demise and to take over caring for Hilda, before his arrest, must indicate that despite his own miserly ways, the man did possess some degree of humanity – little Ernie Grant said that unlike the Vonderahes, Chickie and the Seddons were always nice to him. As Filson Young, compiler of the Seddon volume in the *Notable British Trials* series, eloquently put it, Seddon was convicted not because the Crown succeeded in proving his guilt, but because he failed to prove his innocence.

The trial ended with Seddon being found guilty of the wilful murder of Eliza Mary Barrow and sentenced to death. Mrs Seddon was acquitted. The verdicts were surprising in view of the fact that there was far more evidence against Margaret Seddon than against her husband. Before sentence of death was pronounced Seddon gave a long and powerful speech, quoting facts and figures, and gave a full protestation of his innocence. His lengthy address ended:

> ... You have also referred, my lord, to the letter that I sent to the Vonderahes after her death wherein I omit to state anything at all regarding the money. I thought I pointed out in the witness-box that at that moment when I wrote that letter, the search having been made in the box, there was no money to mention. I had not had the money. The prosecution has never traced the money to me. The prosecution has not traced anything to me in the shape of money, which is the greatest motive suggested by the prosecution in this case for my committing the diabolical crime of which I declare before the Great Architect of the Universe I am not guilty, my lord. Anything more I might have to say I do not suppose will be of any account, but, still, if it is the last words that I speak, I am not guilty of the crime for which I stand committed.

Seddon concluded his speech by raising his hands as if he was taking a freemason's oath. The judge, too, was a freemason. He was moved to tears. Seddon having completed his final address and the judge having assumed the black cap, and the chaplain having been summoned, an usher of the court called out:

> Oyez! Oyez! Oyez! My lords the King's Justices do strictly charge and command all persons to keep silence while sentence of death

is passing upon the prisoner at the bar, upon pain of imprison-ment. God save the King!

Mr Justice Bucknill then addressed Seddon:

Frederick Henry Seddon, you have been found guilty of the wilful murder of Eliza Mary Barrow. With that verdict I am bound to say I agree. I should be more than terribly pained if I thought that I, in my charge to the jury, had stated anything against you that was not supported by the evidence. But even if what you say is strictly correct, that there is no evidence that you ever were left at a material time alone in the room with the deceased person, there is still in my opinion ample evidence to show that you had the opportunity of putting poison into her food or into her medicine. You have a motive for this crime; that motive was the greed of gold. Whether it was that you wanted to put an end to the annuities or not, I know not – you only can know. Whether it was to get the gold that was or was not, but which you thought was in the cash box, I do not know. But I think I do know this, that you wanted to make a great pecuniary profit by felonious means. This murder has been described by yourself in the box as one which, if made out against you, was a barbarous one – a murder of design, a cruel murder. It is not for me to harrow your feelings.

Seddon interjected:

It does not affect me. I have a clear conscience.

Mr Justice Bucknill continued:

I have very little more to say, except to remind you that you have had a very fair and patient trial. Your learned counsel, who has given his undivided time to this case, has done everything that a councel at the English Bar could do. The Attorney-General has conducted this case with remarkable fairness, and the jury have shown a patience and intelligence I have never seen exceeded by any jury with which I have to do. I, as minister of law, have now to pass upon you that sentence which the law demands has to be passed, which is that you have forfeited your life in consequence of your great crime. Try to make peace with your Maker.

Seddon said:

I am at peace.

Mr Justice Bucknill:

> From what you have said, you and I know we both belong to one
> brotherhood, and it is all the more painful to me to have to say
> what I am saying. But our brotherhood does not encourage
> crime; on the contrary, it condemns it. I pray you again to make
> your peace with the Great Architect of the Universe. Mercy –
> pray for it, ask for it. It may be some consolation to you to know
> that I agree with the verdict that the jury has passed with regard
> to your wife. But that does not make it better for you. Whatever
> she has done that was blameworthy in this case, short of any
> criminal offence, if there was anything I feel that she did to help
> you, not to murder, but, it may be, at some time to deal
> improperly with these notes ...

Seddon:

> She done nothing wrong, sir.

Mr Justice Bicknill:

> I am satisfied that the jury has done well and rightly in acquitting
> her. I am satisfied that they have done justice to you. And now I
> have to pass sentence. The sentence of the Court is that you be
> taken from hence to a lawful prison, and from there to a place of
> execution, and that you be there hanged by the neck until you are
> dead; and that your body be buried within the precincts of the
> prison in which you shall have been confined after your con-
> viction; and may the Lord have mercy on your soul!

An appeal was heard on 12 April 1912 and dismissed the following day. There was an enormous public outcry against the
verdict and a petition containing over 250,000 signatures claiming
Seddon's innocence. Despite this overwhelming public support it
was decided that the law must take its course.

Seddon remained interested in money to the end. On the day
before his execution he called for his solicitor to ascertain what
certain articles of his furniture had fetched when sold at auction.
He was concerned that everything possible should be salvaged
from the ruins of his fortune in order to safeguard the future of
his wife and children. When told the relatively small sum of money
the sale had realised, Seddon struck the table and said scorn-
fully, 'That's done it!' He displayed no emotion regarding his
own impending fate. An unprecedented crowd of 7,000 people

gathered outside Pentonville Prison on the day of his execution, 18 April 1912. John Ellis was the executioner.

It seems incredible that Seddon, a man of fastidious habits and meticulous attention to detail, having supposedly poisoned his victim, could make such an elementary mistake in allowing the principal evidence for the crime to remain available for scrutiny by the authorities, that evidence being the body of Miss Eliza Barrow. In Seddon's defence, Mr Marshall Hall pointed out that there was no evidence to prove to the contrary that Miss Barrow, ill with diarrhoea and extremely thirsty, had not accidentally drunk the water in which the flypapers had been soaked and which stood in the saucer near the bed. As Mr Marshall Hall pointed out, 'Why did not Seddon, were he guilty of poisoning Miss Barrow, have the body cremated?' Why not indeed? And if Miss Barrow were indeed murdered, it seems the evidence points to Mrs Seddon as the culprit.

CHAPTER 6

The Infamous Brides in the Bath Murderer

Upper Holloway

1914

This power lay in his eyes ... When he looked at you, you had the feeling that you were being magnetised.

For several years, one of the most notorious criminals in North London's long history, paved a successful path of greed and deceit which led him to commit the ultimate crime of murder on a least three occasions. That he chose to commit his final act of murder in England's capital city was to bring about his downfall. His wife's death was just too unusual not to make a column in a widely read national Sunday newspaper and this set a whole series of events in progress, which once begun, escalated into a massive investigation and brought to justice the man known to history as the 'Brides in the Bath' murderer.

On 18 December 1914, a newly married young woman died in Bismark Road, Upper Holloway, situated to the north of the City of London (and close to the spot where the celebrated Dick Whittington is said to have turned again), just up the road from what was until 1939 Highgate underground station and what is presently known as Archway. The *News of the World* reported the tragedy. This single article on 27 December, on page eleven of just a few lines, and only one column width, brought about the downfall of one of the most infamous wife-killers of all time, George Joseph Smith, the harmonium- playing petty criminal, confidence trickster, antique dealer and serial bigamist.

George Joseph Smith was born on 11 January 1872, at 92 Roman Road, Bethnal Green, in London's East End. When he was just nine-years old he was sentenced to eight years in a reformatory at Gravesend. Such an early introduction to the reality of punishment for wrong doing might possibly have instilled in Smith a total contempt for the law; his subsequent conduct would certainly seem to bear that out. Shortly after his release, at the age of sixteen, Smith found himself in trouble with the law again. On 7 February 1891, he was sentenced at Lambeth Police Court to six months' hard labour for stealing a bicycle. Soon after his release he began a three-year stint in the Northamptonshire Regiment but this period of going straight did not last for long and in 1996 he was sentenced to twelve months' hard labour at North London Sessions for larceny and receiving stolen goods. However, this time he used an alias when charged – George Baker – the first of his many false names. In fact it was one of his numerous lady-friends who had actually done the stealing for him.

Smith had an eye for the ladies and judging by his success in the marital stakes, it would seem the ladies had an eye for him too. It is difficult to imagine from the photographs that exist of this infamous rogue what the attraction was. Clearly Smith possessed sufficient charm and *savoir-faire* to make him irresistible. One of his 'brides', in fact his first bigamous bride, whom he married in 1899 and who survived, described him thus:

> He had an extraordinary power ... This power lay in his eyes ... When he looked at you, you had the feeling that you were being magnetized. They were little eyes that seemed to rob you of your will.

This first bigamous wife is not identifiable by name. Possibly, at some point in the investigation into Smith's background, perhaps at her request, her identity was concealed. Smith may well have possessed the necessary charms to attract numerous females, but he certainly adopted a parsimonious lifestyle once he had made his conquest. He travelled third class, lodged his brides cheaply and took them by bicycle or on foot to places of free public entertainment.

On his release from prison in 1897 he went to Leicester, where he opened a baker's shop at 28 Russell Square. The money he used for this, £115, was stolen for him from her employers by his lady-friend, who had provided such services for Smith before. This time Smith called himself George Oliver Love. It was during his time in Leicester that Smith met Caroline Beatrice Thornhill, an eighteen-year-old maidservant. Her father was a bootmaker.

He strongly disapproved of the twenty-six-year-old suitor who presented himself as his daughter's future husband, but Caroline married her suitor on 17 January 1898 and became Mrs Love. Some years later she described her husband as having:

> Complexion fair, hair brown, ginger moustache, peak chin, on left arm a very large scar, military walk, stands 5 feet 9 inches.

She also said that during the time she knew him she never saw him do any work. Within six months the bakery business had failed. Smith treated his new wife unkindly and often vented his frustration by beating her. Distraught and fearful of her husband, she left and fled to Nottingham. Smith soon followed her, made amends and once again won her over.

George Joseph Smith. John D Murray collection

Smith used his charms to persuade Caroline that they could make a success of their marriage and an easy profit into the bargain. His gullible young wife was taken in and Smith devised a plan. He and Mrs Love moved first to London, where he posed as her employer and gave references to secure her work with various families for whom she was engaged as a maid. She stole from them. Similar scams were perpetrated in Brighton, Hove and Hastings. In the autumn of 1899, while trying to sell some silver spoons she had stolen, Mrs Love was arrested in Hastings. She was given a twelve-month prison sentence; her husband had conveniently disappeared.

Smith's callous abandonment of his wife deeply hurt and angered her. He used the year of his wife's absence to cement a relationship with a middle-aged boarding-house keeper, whom he bigamously married in London and then quickly relieved her of her money before leaving her for pastures new. On her release from prison Mrs Love sought her revenge. She found her husband and successfully incriminated him. On 9 January 1901, Smith was jailed at Hastings for two years for receiving stolen goods. After his release from prison in 1903 he went to Leicester in search of

Caroline, but, fortunately for her, this time Mrs Love had made good her escape by emigrating to Canada, and Smith did not follow her.

Smith then embarked upon wooing an assortment of ladies of means, many of whom succumbed to his charms, some to his bigamous marital bed and three of his six known bigamous wives to a watery death. The full extent of Smith's amorous adventures will never be known. The assortment of one-time besotted and later humiliated ladies, too embarrassed to come forward, may have amounted to a considerable number. The years where little is known about his activities may hold many a sad story and his exploits before 1903 and after 1908 would seem to bear this out.

It was in June 1908 that he met a widow called Florence Wilson. They had a whirlwind courtship lasting three weeks and then married in London. Shortly after the wedding Smith persuaded Florence to withdraw £30 from her post office savings account, which she gave to him. He then took her to the Franco-British Exhibition at White City on 3 July. Having left her sitting comfortably on a bench while he went to get a newspaper, he hurried to their lodgings in Camden, packed her belongings and absconded. Having sold Florence's possessions, he used the money to set himself up in business as a second-hand dealer in Gloucester Road, Bristol. (At this point it is worth mentioning that the £115 he used to set up his bakery business in Leicester in 1897 represented about two years' wages for an average, comfortably well-off working man at that time. Mrs Wilson's £30 was worth more than six months' wages.) The move to Bristol brought Smith into contact with a woman to whom he would remain attached for the rest of his life.

In Bristol Smith advertised for a housekeeper and engaged Edith Mabel Pegler. Romance followed and he married her on 30 July 1908, using his own name. Edith may have been the one true love of his life for he did not rob, dessert or murder her, and returned to her many times with the proceeds of his subsequent 'marriages'. Their business as antiques dealers saw them travelling to Bedford, Luton, Croydon, London and Southend-on-Sea. Smith often went away on business alone and Edith accepted her 'husband's' often extended trips without question. He would communicate with her by letter or postcard and would occasionally send her money. If she ran out of funds during a particularly long absence,

Edith would return to her mother in Bristol. Smith would attribute the sometimes substantial sums he brought home to her to successful business deals. When he told her he had been abroad to Canada or Spain, she believed him entirely.

In October 1909, Smith married his next bride. Calling himself George Rose, he met a spinster clerk named Sarah Freeman in Southampton. He charmed her and convinced her he was a man of means supported by a wealthy aunt. He usually dressed well and his appearance in a frock coat and top hat gave the impression that he was well off. The newly married Mr and Mrs Rose moved to lodgings in London. His latest bride was very keen to help her husband achieve his ambition of having an antiques business and to that end Sarah withdrew her savings, some £260, and also sold some government stock. Once he had obtained her money, she was surplus to requirements. On 5 November Smith took Sarah out for the day; they visited the National Gallery. Whiloe Smith went to the lavatory, his wife waited patiently for him. He never returned. While she waited Smith went back to their lodgings in Clapham, removed her belongings and sold them. Sarah was left with three empty tea chests and a bicycle, totally destitute. In all he had obtained around £400 from her, about four years' wages for the average working man. With the money he brought Edith to Southend, where he established a second-hand furniture shop at 22 Glenmore Street, purchased for £270. He also took out a £30 mortgage on the property and bought a house at 86 Ashley Down Road, Bristol, largely on loan.

Bessie Mundy. John D Murray collection

In 1910, Beatrice (Bessie) Constance Mundy, then living in a boarding house in Clifton, a fashionable Bristol suburb, was a thirty-one-year-old spinster. Her father, who died in 1904, had been a bank manager at Warminster, in Wiltshire and had left his daughter a small fortune held in trust, so the capital could not be touched. It amounted to over £2,500 in gilt-edged securities, administered by a family trust, headed by her uncle. Bessie received a monthly allowance of about £8 – a lesser amount than the funds allowed, but her uncle had a low opinion of her ability to handle money. As a result the trust fund accumulated.

While out walking one day Miss Mundy had a chance meeting with a picture restorer by the name of Henry Williams, otherwise known as George Joseph Smith. Within just a few days Smith had swept Bessie off her feet and they were soon on their way to Weymouth, where they moved into lodgings at 14 Rodwell Avenue. Bessie and Smith were married at Weymouth Registry Office on 26 August 1910, whereupon Bessie wrote:

> Dear Uncle,
> I got married today, my husband is writing tonight.
>
> Yours truly,
> B. Williams

Bessie's husband wrote to her uncle:

> Bessie hopes you will forward as much money as possible at your earliest by registered letter. Am pleased to say Bessie is in perfect health, and we are both looking forward to a bright happy future. Believe me,
>
> Yours faithfully,
> Henry Williams

By the time Smith had got his hands on the accumulated balance in Bessie's trust fund, which amounted to £138, it was 13 December. Having cajoled the money out of her, he promptly left Bessie, but not before writing a letter giving instructions on how to conceal her shame and accusing her of having given him venereal disease:

> Dearest,
> I fear you have blighted all my hopes of a happy future. I have caught from you a disease which is called the bad disorder. For you to be in such a state proves you could not have kept yourself morally clean ... For the sake of my health and honour, and yours too, I must go to London ... to get properly cured of this disease. It will cost me a great deal of money, because it might take years ... Tell the landlady and everyone else that I have gone to France. But tell your uncle the truth ... If he happens to ask you about the money which was sent to you in a yellow bag, say two days after I had gone you happened to go on the beach and

fall asleep and when you woke the bag of money was gone ...
Whatever you do, stick to everything you say. Never alter it or else
you will get mixed up and make a fool of yourself ...

Having achieved his aim of getting hold of some ready cash,
Smith did not go to London but returned to Edith, who was in
Bristol. Bessie left Weymouth and went to live with a friend,
Mrs Sarah Tuckett, in Weston-super-Mare, much nearer to her
former home in Clifton. One morning, during March 1912, Bessie
went out at about eleven o'clock and during her stroll along the
esplanade spotted her husband, Henry Williams. She approached
him, but instead of reprimanding him or reporting him to the
authorities for having absconded with her money, she once again
succumbed to his charms. He told her he had been looking for her
for over a year. Mrs Tuckett said that Bessie returned at about one
o'clock. 'She was very excited.' Smith called at Bessie's lodgings at
about three o'clock. Mrs Tuckett took an instant dislike to Smith,
but Bessie told her that she had forgiven her husband and had
decided to go back to him and they had already consulted a
solicitor. Mrs Tuckett told Smith that it was her duty to wire
Bessie's aunt to come at once. However, Bessie left that afternoon
with Smith and promised to return in the evening. She did not take
her belongings. Mrs Tuckett never saw her again.

Bessie and Smith went from town to town while he made
enquiries as to how he might legally take possession of her fortune.
In May the couple rented a property at 80 High Street Herne Bay,
where Smith set up a brass plate proclaiming that he was an
antiques dealer. By then he had discovered that if Bessie made a
will in her husband's favour, in the event of her death he would
inherit her fortune. Bessie's fate was sealed. On Monday 8 July,
separate wills were drawn up, each in the other's favour. On 9 July,
the couple bought a second-hand zinc bath and Bessie herself beat
down the price from £2 to £1 17s 6d. This was the bath in which
she was to die.

Smith then set about a process he was to repeat with two
subsequent brides. He set about convincing Bessie that she was
not well. On Wednesday 10 July, Smith took Bessie to visit the
recently qualified Dr French. He told the doctor that his wife had
suffered a fit. However, all Bessie complained of was a headache.
At 1.30am, on Friday 12 July, Dr French was called to 80 High
Street, because Mrs Williams had suffered another fit. He could

find nothing particularly wrong with her. It was a warm night and Mrs Williams was in bed, looking as if she had just woken up. The doctor prescribed a sedative. The next afternoon, the doctor saw the Williamses taking a walk and all appeared to be well. On the same day Bessie wrote to her uncle at the suggestion of her husband and she told him about the fits.

On the morning of Saturday 13 July, at a little after 7.00am, Bessie prepared to have a bath in one of the upstairs spare rooms, and made numerous journeys carrying buckets of water from the kitchen. Her husband went out to buy some fish. Bessie, with her hair in curling pins, got into the bath. Some time afterwards her husband returned. At about eight o'clock, Dr French received a note from Mr Williams:

Can you come at once? I'm afraid my wife is dead!

On his arrival at 80 High Street Dr French discovered the body of Mrs Williams in a bath in an upstairs room. The body was naked and partly submerged, her legs were resting out of the water on the end of the bath and in her right hand she was clutching a bar of soap. Dr French informed the police of the fatality and later that morning Police Constable Kitchingham took a statement from the widower. Bessie's body had been laid on the floor near the bath in which she had died and during the afternoon a woman came to lay her out.

Smith sent a wire to Bessie's uncle:

Bessie died in fit this morning. Letter following.

Smith then wrote a letter explaining how shocked he was at the loss of his dear wife and gave an account of the circumstances of her death in the bath. No post-mortem examination was carried out on Bessie Mundy's body. An inquest was held on Monday 15 July and the bereaved husband wept throughout. Dr French stated that in his opinion the woman drowned as a result of a fit of epilepsy in the bath. The jury returned a verdict of misadventure:

... the cause of death being that while taking a bath she had an epileptic seizure causing her to fall back in the water and be drowned.

At 2.30pm, on Tuesday 16 July, Bessie was buried in a common grave. Smith had arranged the funeral before any of her relatives had the chance to make arrangements to attend. Smith never paid for the bath in which Bessie Mundy died. Having obtained credit, he returned it to the ironmonger's six days later. It had served its purpose and was of no further use to him.

Bessie Mundy's estate was proved at £2,571 and, as Smith had arranged, under the terms of her will her 'husband' inherited it all. Despite her relatives' attempts to contest the will, Bessie's money had been paid to her sole executor and legatee, Henry Williams. Smith opened several bank accounts and used some of the money to purchase seven houses in Bristol and an annuity that brought him £76 a year. While all Bessie's affairs were being wound up, Smith remained active elsewhere. During the month after Bessie's death, August 1912, Smith contacted Edith Peglar and told her to join him in Margate. Before he disappeared again in 1913, Smith and Edith moved first to Tunbridge Wells, then to Bristol, Weston-Super-Mare and finally back to Bristol. (Edith's account of her relationship with Smith indicated that it was not an unhappy one, although she stated that he did beat her from time to time.)

In October 1913, Smith was once again on the coast, at Southsea in Hampshire. He was, as usual, on the prowl for a new bride. Alice Burnham was a buxom, twenty-five-year-old private nurse who looked after an elderly male invalid. Smith spotted her praying in a Wesleyan chapel. Romance quickly followed and Smith married her at Portsmouth registry office on 4 November – but not before discovering that she was not without means and that her father, a fruit grower from Buckinghamshire, was looking after £104 for her. Miss Burnham's father Charles met Smith before the marriage took place and took a thorough dislike to him. At this marriage ceremony Smith once again used his real name.

He wrote to Alice's father suggesting that her money should be handed over, but her father was anxious to know more about his new son-in-law's background and proceeded to investigate. When Smith heard about this by letter he replied to his father-in-law with a postcard, which was read out at the trial:

Sir,

In answer to your application regarding my parentage, my mother was a bus-horse, my father a cab-driver, my sister a roughrider over the Artic regions. My brothers were all gallant sailors on a steam-roller. This is the only information I can give to those who are not entitled to ask such questions contained in the letter I received on the 24th inst.

Your despised son-in-law

G. Smith

Smith got Alice's £104 from her reluctant father after he engaged the services of a solicitor. He also persuaded her to withdraw £27 9s 5d from her savings bank. He had already taken out a life insurance policy on his wife's life for £500, on 3 November, the day before the marriage took place. Alice made out a will in her husband's favour and Smith decided to take his new bride on an out-of-season holiday to the Lancashire resort of Blackpool. They arrived there on 10 December. First, they visited a boarding house in Adelaide Street, but decided not to stay because it lacked a bathroom. They eventually settled on a establishment run by Mrs Crossley at 16 Regent Road, which did have a bathroom. The rent was 10s a week.

Smith expressed concern for his wife's health to Mrs Crossley and Dr Billing was consulted. The long journey from the south coast to Blackpool had been an arduous and tiring experience

Alice Burnham. John D Murray collection

for his wife: she had a headache. Dr Billing could find no cause except mild constipation. Smith persuaded Alice to write to her parents:

> My husband does all he can for me, in fact I have the best husband in the world . . .

In the early evening, two days after their arrival in Blackpool, Mr and Mrs Smith went out for a walk. It was Friday 12 December 1913, the last night of Alice Burnham's life. The daughter of the landlady had agreed to prepare a bath for Mrs Smith, and the couple returned to their lodgings a little after 8.00pm. At 8.15pm, the Crossleys were sitting in their kitchen, which was under the bathroom, when they noticed water stains appearing on the ceiling and down one of the walls. They assumed the bath had run over. At that moment Smith appeared at the kitchen door in a breathless state. He had two eggs in his hand. He told Mrs Crossley:

I've brought these for our breakfast.

Having been told about the water, Smith went upstairs and a few moments later was heard to call out:

Fetch the doctor! My wife cannot speak to me!

Dr Billing was sent for and after he had made his examination, he returned downstairs to where Joseph Crossley and his wife were anxiously waiting and told them:

Oh, she is drowned – she is dead.

Mrs Crossley found the tragedy, and Mr Smith's apparent indifference to it, too much to cope with. She arranged for him to stay next door that night. The next day he returned to make the necessary arrangements. In the afternoon, Smith played Mrs Crossley's piano and drank a bottle of whisky.

The inquest was held at 6.30pm and Smith wept throughout. The coroner's jury returned a verdict of accidental death. Much to Mrs Crossley's surprise and disgust, Smith arranged for as cheap a funeral as possible. Alice's body was placed in a plain deal coffin and given a pauper's funeral, which took place at noon on Monday 15 December. Mrs Crossley was outraged when Smith callously remarked:

When they are dead, they are done with.

Smith left for Southsea shortly after the funeral. As he departed, Mrs Crossley, who didn't like his manner and thought he was a very hard-hearted man, shouted after him, 'Crippen'.

Smith sold all of Alice's belongings that had been left in their lodgings in Southsea and returned to Edith in Bristol. He also pocketed the £500 paid out on the life insurance policy he had taken out on Alice. Among other benefits, the proceeds he received as a result of his involvement with Alice Burnham enabled him to increase his annuity by £30 a year. Having settled matters concerning the affairs of yet another 'bride', Smith returned to Bristol where he spent Christmas with Edith and her family. He told Edith he had just returned from a profitable visit to Spain. Early in 1914, Smith and Edith visited London, Cheltenham and Torquay.

Smith also paid a visit to Bath in June, where he adopted the pseudonym John Lloyd and first encountered the lady who was the most high-born and last of his 'brides'.

At the outbreak of the First World War, on 4 August, Smith was staying with Edith at Ashley Road, Bournemouth. It was during this time, that he, while dressed in white flannels, white boots and a boater, and listening to a band in the sea-front gardens, encountered a maidservant by the name of Alice Reavil. This time he called himself Charles Oliver James. She fell for his charms and they were married in Woolwich by special licence on 17 September. They went to London and took lodgings at 8 Hafer Road, Battersea Rise. He soon persuaded Alice to part with her £76 savings, which she withdrew from the Post Office. He then took her out, left her in some public gardens on the pretext of going to the lavatory, promptly went to their lodgings and took everything except the clothes she was wearing. He immediately went back to Edith in Bournemouth. He gave some of Alice's clothes to Edith, telling her that he had bought them at a sale in London. Smith and Edith then travelled to Bristol, before he returned to what is believed to have been his final victim, the lady whom he had met in Bath in June that year.

Margaret (Peggy) Lofty was the thirty-eight-year-old spinster daughter of a long-deceased clergyman. He introduced himself to her as John Lloyd, estate agent. She was at that time a lady's companion, a position she undertook from time to time, working for various respectable elderly women in the Bristol area. Her employment in that capacity ended in July. Peggy lived in Bath with her sister and elderly mother. She had experienced a deep disappointment earlier that year when she discovered that her fiancée was already married. When Smith, in the guise of John Lloyd appeared on the scene, she must have felt greatly relieved – perhaps she was not going to be 'left on the shelf' after all. He charmed her and told her he would return, and he was as good as his word.

Margaret (Peggy) Lofty.
John D Murray collection

On 15 December, Peggy Lofty left her home to go out for tea, but she never returned. She told none of her family about her intentions to marry Mr Lloyd. Perhaps her previous experience made her reluctant to do so, until the knot had actually been tied. Smith married Miss Lofty at Bath Register Office, on 17 December, having visited London a few days previously to arrange accommodation. They left Bath immediately after the wedding ceremony and took the train to London.

On their arrival in London, the Lloyds went straight to 16 Orchard Road, Highgate, where they intended to lodge. Smith had visited Mrs Heiss, the landlady, a few days previously. However, having had time for reflection following her visit, Mrs Heiss had had second thoughts about taking the Lloyds in. He had inspected the rooms and the bath. Mrs Heiss, a German lady, later commented:

I did not like the way he asked about the bath . . . He measured it with his eyes . . .

She remembered that he remarked that it was a bit small, then said:

I daresay it is large enough for someone to lie in.

She did not like his manner and thought he might be a difficult man to deal with, and this was not a time to have added difficulties if they were avoidable – after all, being German in London in 1914 was not easy. So, when the Lloyds called on 17 December, she told them the rooms were not ready and turned them away, despite Smith's protests.

However, he was familiar with that area of London and found lodgings in which he and his new wife could spend their wedding night. They moved into two furnished rooms at 14 Bismarck Road. The road was – and still is, albeit with a different name, situated opposite the Whittington Hospital and traverses the hillside between Highgate Hill and Archway Road. Bismarck, like many German names, was deemed unpopular both during and in the aftermath of the First World War, and the title was altered to Waterlow Road. The house had a bath. Miss Louisa Blatch was the landlady. That evening, Mr Lloyd took his wife to see Dr Bates at 30 Archway Road. Characteristically for Smith, the dutiful husband expressed his concern to the doctor about his dear wife's poor state of health. The following morning, Friday 18 December, the last day of Peggy Lofty's life, Smith took his new bride to a solicitor to make her will. Her life was already insured for £700. He also took her on a visit to the Post Office to withdraw her savings. She wrote to her mother informing her of her marriage. She described her husband as:

> ... a thoroughly Christian man ... I have every proof of his love for me ... He has been honourable and kept his word in everything. He is such a nice man ...

Shortly after 7.30pm that evening, Mrs Lloyd took a bath. Miss Blatch, who was ironing in the kitchen, heard splashing coming from the bathroom directly above. She also heard Mr Lloyd playing *Nearer My God To Thee* on the harmonium in the Lloyd's sitting room. Shortly after that, the front door slammed. Miss Blatch said at the trial:

> I heard a sound from the bathroom. It was a sound of splashing. Then there was a noise as of someone putting wet hands or arms on the side of the bath, and then a sigh ... a sort of sound like a child might make.

About ten minutes after Miss Blatch had heard the splashing, the doorbell rang. When she answered it, Mr Lloyd was standing on the doorstep. He mentioned the key which she had given him, but which he had forgotten. He told her that he had been for some tomatoes for Mrs Lloyd's supper and asked if his wife was down from the bathroom yet. He called to her and when his wife didn't answer he went up the stairs. Then he called out to Mrs Blatch:

> My God! It's my wife! She doesn't answer! I do hope nothing has happened to her!

Naturally, when Mr Lloyd entered the bathroom he found that his wife was dead. He tried to resuscitate her but to no avail.

Mrs Lloyd, the former Miss Margaret Lofty, was buried on Monday 21 December and Smith was soon back in Bristol, where he spent Christmas with Edith. On 27 December 1914, a short article appeared in the popular Sunday newspaper the *News of the World*. It was headlined:

Found Dead in Bath.
Bride's Tragic Fate on Day after Wedding

Joseph Crossley, husband of the Smith's landlady in Blackpool, and Charles Burnham from Buckinghamshire, Alice Burnham's father, read the account and thought it sounded suspiciously like the so-called accidental death of Mrs Alice Smith at 16 Regent Road, Blackpool, a little over a year ago, on 13 December 1913. They reported the matter both to their local police and to Scotland Yard. Mrs Heiss, of 16 Orchard Road, Highgate, the landlady who had turned the Lloyds away, also contacted the police. She remembered Smith's comments concerning the size of the bath when he had first inspected her premises.

The inquest was held on New Year's Day, Saturday 1 January 1915. Once again the grieving husband displayed great emotion and he was, of course, exonerated of any blame. The verdict was accidental death. However, as a result of the information given to the police by Joseph Crossley, Charles Burnham and Mrs Heiss, Mr Lloyd was placed under close observation and the police travelled to various parts of the country making exhaustive enquiries during the four weeks that followed. The net was closing in on Smith. The police investigation revealed sufficient evidence to enable them eventually to amass an astonishing 264 exhibits to show to the jury at the trial, and no fewer than 112 witnesses were called.

On 4 January 1915, Smith, calling himself John Lloyd, called at 60 Uxbridge Road, Shepherd's Bush, to consult with his solicitor, Mr Davies. He instructed the lawyer to have his wife's will proved and to realise the proceeds of her life insurance policy. He was completely unaware of the enormous police investigation that was taking place When Smith went to his solicitor's in Shepherd's Bush on 1 February to prove the will, he was arrested outside the building by Chief Inspector Neil and two police sergeants. Having admitted that he was George Joseph Smith, who had married Alice Burnham, he was then charged with bigamy. The same day, Margaret Lofty's body was exhumed and examined by Dr Bernard Spilsbury who, following several high-profile cases, had become the Home Office's honorary pathologist. Dr Spilsbury later travelled to Blackpool and Herne Bay to examine the exhumed bodies of Alice Burnham and Bessie Mundy.

After Smith had been identified by Charles Burnham as the man who had married his daughter, he was remanded in custody. During several appearances at Bow Street Magistrates' Court he shouted abuse at the witnesses and lawyers. Following further

police investigations, Smith was charged on 23 March with the
wilful murder of Bessie Mundy, Alice Burnham and Margaret
Lofty, although he was actually indicted only for the killing of
Bessie Mundy.

At the age of forty three, George Joseph Smith stood in the dock
at the Old Bailey on Tuesday 22 June 1915. His trial lasted nine
days, concluding on 1 July. He pleaded not guilty. During the case,
the sensational revelations reported by the press acted as a diver-
sion from the horrors that were occurring in the trenches across the
English Channel. The presiding judge was Mr Justice Scrutton
and the senior prosecuting counsel was Archibald Bodkin, who
later became Director of Public Prosecutions. Smith was defended
by the formidable Edward Marshall Hall KC. Smith satisfied the
authorities that he had no money and as a consequence Marshall
Hall provided his services for the maximum fee allowed by the
Poor Prisoner's Defence Act, £3 5s 6d.

Archibald Bodkin prosecuting first addressed the jury:

> This case is of a very grave character, and one to which you will
> give the most earnest attention in the interests not only of the
> prisoner, but also of the public.

He then turned his attention to the judge and told him he wished
to discuss an important point of law concerning the admissibility
of certain evidence. Mr Justice Scrutton directed the jury to retire
while it was being argued. This point in the case marked a land-
mark in English criminal law: a precedent was set. Mr Marshall
Hall knew from the documents in his brief that Smith had married
two other women who had both died in their baths, having both
previously made wills with Smith as sole beneficiary. To allow
this information to be admitted would give Smith virtually no
chance of an acquittal and Mr Bodkin wanted to present the evidence. Strong arguments were proffered on both sides. Mr Bodkin
maintained that the prosecution was entitled to call evidence of
any character tending to prove that this was a case of killing by
deliberate design and not by accident. He also suggested that
Smith had employed a 'system'. Mr Marshall Hall contended that
the evidence of a 'system' was admissible only where it was necessary for the defence to set up a denial of intent. In this particular
case, as the prosecution had not put forward sufficient evidence to
displace the primary presumption of innocence in the prisoner, the
inclusion of the evidence of the previous two fatalities was not

necessary. Having considered both arguments, Mr Justice Scrutton ruled that such evidence was admissible. He then recalled the jury and informed them that they must not use this evidence to infer that the prisoner was a man of bad character and infamous acts, but only to help them to decide whether Miss Mundy's death was the result of an accident or had been deliberately engineered by the accused. Mr Bodkin then outlined the facts of the two additional fatalities for which he suggested that the prisoner was responsible.

The evidence given by Dr Spilsbury made it even more difficult for Mr Marshall Hall to proffer his usually masterly defence. He stated that it would have been impossible for his client to have killed Bessie Mundy without leaving some evidence that suggested there had been a struggle or some marks of violence on her. He commented:

If you tried to drown a kitten, it would scratch you, and do you think a woman would not scratch?

In the witness box, Dr Spilsbury said:

If a woman of the stature of Miss Mundy was in the bath in which she died, the first onset of an epileptic fit would stiffen and extend the body. In view of her height, 5 feet 7 inches, I do not think her head would be submerged during that stage of the fit . . . After the seizure had passed the state of the body is that of relaxation. The body would probably be limp and unconscious. Bearing in mind the length of the body and the size of the bath, I do not think she would be likely to be immersed during the state of relaxation . . . Dr French has described her legs straight out from the hips and the feet up against the end of the bath, out of the water. I cannot give any explanation of how a woman – assuming she had an epileptic seizure – could get into that position herself

Mr Marshall Hall had very little evidence at his disposal with which he could adequately defend Smith. He cross-examined Dr Spilsbury with regard to Miss Mundy clutching a bar of soap as she died, suggesting that this could indeed indicate that she had suffered an epileptic seizure. However, Dr Spilsbury was cautious in his reply: 'It's not impossible,' he agreed, before adding, 'but not very likely.' Dr Spilsbury's skills in forensic pathology, a relatively new form of criminal detection, seemed to allow little doubt in the minds of the jury, and his suggestion for the method of drowning Smith might have adopted, added weight to the

overwhelming amount of circumstantial evidence against him. Dr Spilsbury
explained that the vagus nerve, which
connects the brain to the heart, can be
stimulated by a sudden rush of water
into the nose and throat, sending a
message to the heart to stop beating,
and resulting in rapid unconsciousness
and death. The position of the bodies in
the bath in which they were found, and
in particular that of Bessie Mundy,
indicated to him exactly how Smith had
brought about a quick death to his
victims with little sign of struggle.

To prove Dr Spilsbury's theory,
Inspector Neil arranged for a demonstration in an ante-room at the Old
Bailey. The inspector had a nurse,
dressed in a bathing costume, sit in a
bath of water, the bath being of a

Edward Marshall Hall.
Author's collection

similar size and shape to those used by Smith. A police officer
then demonstrated the technique suggested by Dr Spilsbury. He
placed his right hand on the nurse's head and his left arm beneath
both of her knees. The police officer then raised his left arm suddenly while at the same time used his right hand to press down
on the head, pushing it beneath the water. As predicted, Dr
Spilsbury's theory proved correct and a near tragedy resulted. The
nurse had to be revived using artificial respiration.

Mr Marshall Hall was up against mounting evidence, but he
called on all the resources at his disposal. In particular, he stressed
the mutual affection between the prisoner and Edith Pegler, citing
it as evidence of Smith's humanity. Of the 112 witnesses called
at the trial, Edith was the only surviving 'bride' to give evidence.
When she was on the stand, Smith showed signs of distress. She
told the court that the prisoner had on the whole been kind to her.
She said that Smith had warned her of the danger women face
when taking baths. She stated he had told her:

> I should advise you to be careful about these things, as it is known
> that women often lose their lives through weak hearts and
> fainting in the bath.

In his summing up to the jury, Mr Bodkin said:

> In each case you get the simulated marriage ... In each case all
> the ready money the woman had is realized ... In each case
> the woman made a will in the prisoner's favour ... In each
> case the property could only be got at through the woman's death
> ... In each case the prisoner is the first to discover the death ... In
> each case the prisoner is the person in immediate association
> with each woman before her death ... In each case the bathroom
> doors are either unfastenable or unfastened ... In each case there
> is the immediate disappearance of the prisoner.

Circumstantial evidence, perhaps, but convincing nevertheless.

Mr Justice Scrutton's summing up lasted almost an entire day
and during it Smith interrupted several times, at one point
shouting:

> You'll have me hung the way you are going on! – Sentence me
> and have done with it! ... It is a disgrace to a Christian country! I
> am not a murderer – though I may be a bit peculiar.

The judge also made specific reference to contemporary events.
He said:

> Since last August all over Europe thousands of lives of com-
> batants, sometimes of non-combatants, have been taken daily,
> with no warning, and in many cases with no justification ... And
> yet, while this wholesale destruction of human life is going on, for
> some days all the apparatus of justice in England has been
> considering whether the prosecution are right in saying that one
> man should die.

The jury retired at 2.52pm on 1 July and took just twenty-two
minutes to find George Joseph Smith guilty. Before he passed
sentence of death by hanging, Mr Justice Scruton remarked:

> Judges sometimes use this occasion to warn the public against the
> repetition of such crimes – they sometimes use such occasions to
> exhort the prisoner to repentance. I propose to take neither of
> these courses. I do not believe there is another man in England
> who needs to be warned against the commission of such a crime,
> and I think that exhortation to repentance would be wasted on
> you.

The execution of George Joseph Smith. Illustrated Police News

Pale-faced and sweating profusely, Smith gripped the dock tightly as the death sentence was passed on him. He then leaned over the dock and said to Edward Marshall Hall:

I thank you Mr Marshall Hall, for everything you have done. I have great confidence in you. I shall bear up.

After sentence had been passed on Smith, Edith Peglar burst into tears as she left the Old Bailey.

An appeal was lodged, but dismissed. Smith was then removed to Maidstone Prison from Pentonville, where he had been incarcerated since his last committal. It was there, on a sunny morning, at eight o'clock on Friday 13 August 1915, that he was taken across the prison yard to the execution shed and hanged by John Ellis. He was in a state of collapse on the scaffold and maintained that he was innocent of murder to the end. After the execution, the body of George Joseph Smith was formally identified by Inspector Neil. It was then buried in a pit of quicklime within the confines of Maidstone Prison.

CHAPTER 7

The 1920s through to the 1950s

The Body in the Bathtub, Regents Park, 1922

Mrs Alice Hilda Middleton was the wife of a merchant seaman, who was on a long voyage to the Far East. Mrs Middleton took lodgings while her husband was at sea and in the early summer of 1922 she went to lodge with Cecil Maltby, a forty-seven-year-old tailor, who lived above his shop at 24 Park Road, a street that runs from Lord's cricket ground to the top of Baker Street. Although Maltby had inherited his father's successful business, he had become a heavy drinker and allowed business to decline to the point of bankruptcy. Separated from his wife and children, following Mrs Middleton's arrival he clearly gained some relief from his alcoholic despair, neglecting his business affairs even further to spend a great deal of time attending race meetings with her. Mrs Middleton was not seen alive again after August. When her husband returned from his sea voyage in December 1922 he reported her missing.

Police made enquiries, which led them to Maltby. He did not allow them entry into his living quarters but told them Mrs Middleton had left him on 15 August. The place smelled abominably, and all his utility services had been cut off. The police decided to watch the premises as neighbours informed them that Maltby had effectively barricaded himself in and would not allow anyone access, nor had he left the premises for months. Increasing complaints about the worsening sanitary conditions resulted in a health order being issued, on 10 January 1923, which allowed the authorities to break in. The police entered the premises from both the front and rear of the shop. On reaching the first floor living quarters they heard a single shot. Maltby was found lying dead in a bedroom, shot through the mouth. The entire place was in a disgustingly filthy state. Worse still, in the kitchen, was a bath that had been boarded over and used as a dining table. Inside the bath, wrapped in a sheet, were found the decomposing remains of Mrs

Middleton. Attached to the sheet was a note, saying:

> In Memory of darling Pat, who committed suicide on 24 August
> 1922, 8.30am.

Maltby had left several letters implying that on 24 August he
had struggled with Mrs Middleton who was threatening to shoot
herself and during the struggle to take the gun from her it went
off. However, a post-mortem examination of Alice Middleton's
remains revealed that she had three bullet wounds in her back, and
the bullets had struck her body while she was in either a sitting or
lying position. At the inquest on the body of Mrs Middleton, the
jury returned a verdict of murder and *felo de se*, stating that Cecil
Maltby was in a sound state of health and mind and took his own
life to avoid the consequences of his act.

One-legged Murdering Lover, Camden Town, 1926

On New Year's Day 1926, in a house in Arlington Road, Camden
Town, seventeen-year-old Polly Edith Walker was discovered
lying beneath her bed in her nightdress, by her widowed mother.
She had been strangled with one of her own silk stockings by
her twenty-five-year-old, French Canadian, one-legged street
musician lover Ewen Stitchell, aso known as Eugene de Vere. In
addition to being strangled, Polly had also sustained several head
injuries. A copper-handled poker was found lying on the blood-
soaked eiderdown, as were some broken fire tongs. Stitchell had a
charismatic personality but lived life almost like a vagrant. Polly
was attracted to him and felt sorry for him and had taken him
under her wing. Following his arrest at Hitchin in Hertfordshire,
on Sunday 3 January, Stitchell admitted killing Polly. He said he
had done so out of jealousy having discovered that she had taken
another lover. *The Times* reported that, despite his artificial leg,
Stitchell is believed to have walked the thirty-two miles to Hitchin,
following the murder. Ewen Stitchell was hanged at Pentonville on
24 March 1926.

The Body in the Burning Shed, Camden Town, 1933

On the evening of Tuesday 3 January 1933, a garden shed at
30 Hawley Crescent, Camden Town, was the scene of a murder

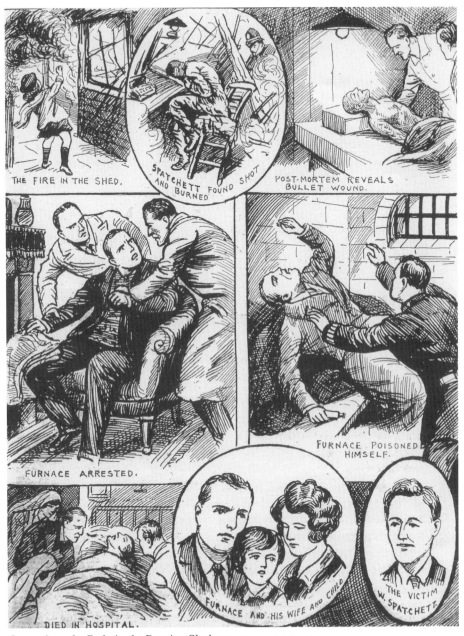

THE FIRE IN THE SHED.

SPATCHETT FOUND SHOT AND BURNED

POST-MORTEM REVEALS BULLET WOUND.

FURNACE ARRESTED.

FURNACE. POISONED HIMSELF.

DIED IN HOSPITAL.

FURNACE AND HIS WIFE AND CHILD

THE VICTIM W. SPATCHETT

Scenes from the Body in the Burning Shed case. Illustrated Police News the perpetrator had attempted to disguise as his own suicide. Inside the partially burned shed, sitting at a desk, were the charred remains of a man's body. The shed, which was divided into two portions, had been rented as an office by unsuccessful business-man, builder and decorator, forty-two-year-old Samuel Furnace. A suicide note meant to create the impression that the body was that of Furnace read: 'Goodbye all. No work. No money. Sam J. Furnace.'

However, suspicion was aroused when a bullet wound was discovered in the corpse's back and the teeth of the deceased were of a man considerably younger than Furnace. A post-mortem examination revealed that the dead man had been shot twice. Further investigation showed him to be a twenty-five-year-old rent collector, Walter Spatchett, who lived with his parents in Dartmouth Park Road, Highgate. Enquiries revealed that Furnace and Spatchett were well acquainted and often met socially to play billiards. On the day before the fire, Spatchett had collected £36 in rent payments.

A nationwide hunt was instigated for Furnace. Walter Spatchett was buried at Highgate Cemetery on 11 January. Furnace was caught after he contacted his brother-in-law, Charles Tuckfield, by letter, date stamped 14 January, requesting that he bring some clean shirts and other items of clothing to a location in Essex. The police were informed immediately and that same day, 15 January, Furnace was apprehended at a lodging house, at 11 Whitegate Road, Southend. Furnace was brought back to Kentish Town police station. He claimed that the killing had been accidental. Locked in a cell overnight, he asked if he could have his overcoat, as it was particularly cold. When the coat was brought to him he took out a phial of hydrochloric acid which he had secreted in the lining and drank the contents. He was taken to St Pancras Hospital where doses of morphine were administered to ease his suffering, but he never regained consciousness and died about twenty-four hours later, on Tuesday 17 January. His body was taken to St Pancras Mortuary where a post-mortem examination was carried out by Home Office pathologist Sir Bernard Spilsbury. On Friday 20 January, a coroner's jury concluded that Walter Spatchett's death was not accidental and that Samuel James Furnace was guilty of his murder.

Gunman Shoots Himself Dead after Shooting Vicar, Stamford Hill, 1937

St John's Church Hall, situated in Vartry Road, Stamford Hill was the scene of an amazing drama during May 1937. Mr W E Longhurst, the verger, entered the hall first and was shot at by a man who was hiding behind the stage curtains and using the back of a chair as a gun rest. Two shots whizzed past him but each missed. As this was happening, the sixty-two-year-old vicar, the Rev Charles Walter Sykes, arrived at the scene. He immediately went to investigate and no sooner had he got through the doorway than he was shot in the face. Rev Sykes staggered backwards and fell down the steps leading to the hall. Mr Longhurst knelt beside the injured clergyman and tried to stem the flow of blood. He also shouted for help. A postman, Mr Frederick Lake, who was passing, heard the cries and rushed to see what was happening. He discovered the vicar lying in a pool of blood. When Mr Lake went to enter the hall, Rev Sykes called out weakly:

Don't go in.

Mr Longhurst described the events:

I had entered the hall when I was suddenly startled by the sound of a shot. At the same time a voice said, 'stand still. Do not move.' I replied, 'All right, what's the matter?' and just afterwards took three steps backwards. Then there was another shot and the command was repeated. I could not see, but from a burst of flame I noticed that he was firing from behind curtains at the side of the stage. I took a chance, ducked down, and zig-zagged down the hall. As I reached the door a third shot rang out. Fortunately it missed me, and I was able to get to safety. I yelled to passers by, and one of them ran to the vicarage. The vicar came along a passage from the church. Before we could stop him he advanced round the door into the hall, and as he did so there was a shot. A bullet struck him in the jaw. I crawled towards him, and then the postman came, and I called to him for help.

Mr Frederick Lake, the postman said:

I came into Vartry Road and heard cries for help coming from the Parish hall. I hurried forward, and was just going into the doorway when I saw the vicar lying there. As I was about to enter the hall a shot rang out. I dodged back and then there was another shot.

Mr Lake entered the porchway and as a bullet screamed past him, he ducked for cover. Courageously, he dashed forward, slammed the doors of the hall to and locked the gunman in. Mr Longhurst called for help, and while he did all he could for the wounded vicar, a passer-by was sent to telephone for the police.

Moments after the doors to the church hall had been locked a shot was heard. When the police were called they sped to the scene in cars and tenders. They entered the church hall and there they found a man dead with a .22 target rifle beside him. He had shot himself through the mouth. He was identified as Alfred Stanley Kirby, a twenty-five-year-old printer, of Derwent Avenue, Edmonton. He had been a churchwarden and member of St John's Church Scout troupe. His family had moved to Edmonton a year previously and he then gave up his duties. When the police arrived the vicar was found weak from loss of blood and suffering severely from shock. He was taken to the Prince of Wales Hospital, Tottenham, where he died.

Prostitute's Body found in Warehouse Cellar, Islington, 1937

In 1937, Frederick George Murphy lived in Islington, at 57a Colebrooke Row and worked for Harding's, a furnishing company, at 22 The Green, Islington. On 14 May, he informed his employers that he had discovered the body of a woman in the cellar of their warehouse. When the police arrived to investigate, Murphy had already left the scene. The dead woman was identified as a well-known prostitute, Rosina Field. She had been strangled. Mrs Field habitually took a room at 13 Duncan Terrace and had last done so on 11 May.

When Frederick Murphy turned up at Poplar police station the next day he had bloodstains on his clothes. Declaring himself completely innocent and wishing to clear himself, he made a long statement. He told the police he had been on a pub crawl at the time Field was killed and listed various pubs he had visited. This statement was later contradicted after witnesses said they had seen Murphy enter the warehouse with Rosina Field, at the time he claimed to have been drinking elsewhere. This was not the only time that Murphy had been linked to a murdered prostitute. He had been accused of murder previously when he had been seen in the company of Katherine Peck, known as 'Carbolic Kate', shortly before she had been found in Aldgate with her throat cut. On that occasion, Murphy had been fortunate, as the main witness for the prosecution disappeared. This time however, he was not so lucky. He was tried at the Old Bailey before the Lord Chief Justice, Lord Hewart and found guilty of the murder of Rosina Field. In his summing up Lord Hewart asked the jury if they could have any doubt on the evidence of the three witnesses for the Crown, either that Murphy was acquainted with Mrs Field, or upon the crucial point or that he was with her at the critical time on Coronation Day. There was a blank in his account of his movements between 8.00pm and 9.00pm on that day, and the jury might think the fullness of details he had given about other times supplied a commentary on the blank. If they accepted the prosecution's evidence, that was the period when Mrs Field met her death. Commenting on Murphy's story that he did not inform the police because he thought they were 'up against him,' Lord Hewart said:

> Can you accept that story? Can you believe that an innocent man would have concealed his discovery from the police because he was afraid that would start a charge against him?

Before sentence of death was passed, when he was asked if he had anything to say, Murphy said: 'Yes.' Speaking loudly for about five minutes, he alleged perjury by witnesses, made accusations against the police, and protested his innocence. During his outburst Murphy in addressing Lord Hewart, said:

> ... you could not give a good word for me. You told the jury that I was nothing else but a liar ... I can prove to you that Rosie Keen [a witness who had given evidence] had been in that shop with me. I want my counsel to go there and find out if some bedding has been sold. That will show that she had been there. I can also say that I have witnesses to prove that men have been in the shop with Rosie Keen. If anyone ever committed perjury in a case it is Rosie Keen and Divisional Detective Inspector Salisbury. When I was arrested the inspector said to me, 'Murphy, I don't want to be hard on you. Say you hit this woman and I will break this charge down to manslaughter.' I said, 'It has nothing to do with me, and I know nothing about it.' ... Chief Inspector Bennett

came in [actually Superintendent], and Salisbury said, 'Do you want to say anything to him? I said, 'No.' They undressed me in the police station in front of fifteen officers. I was there naked for a quarter of an hour. I said to Salisbury, 'Have I got to stay like this?' and they gave me a blanket . . . Mrs Marshall tells you I said I was going to bury the body. Why didn't she say it in the police court? She only said it here. Don't you think in your summing up you should have asked more about Rosie Keen. You just think a minute. It is very near time that committing perjury in these courts was put a stop to. It is not the first time but several times where perjury has been committed in different names and in murder trials at that.

The Lord Chief Justice then asked Murphy if he had anything further to say, to which Murphy replied he had nothing. In passing sentence of death, his lordship told Murphy:

> The jury on clear and compelling evidence have convicted you of the crime of wilful murder. You know as well as I know that the verdict is right.

Murphy showed no fear of the hangman's rope while he awaited his execution at Pentonville. He laughed and joked with the warders and refused the ministrations of a Roman Catholic priest. By coincidence, the inquests on the victim Mrs Field and on Murphy was held on the same day. That of the victim at St Pancras Coroner's Court, and that on Murphy at Pentonville Prison. Mr W Bentely Purchase, the St Pancras coroner, after formal proceedings said he would record a verdict 'that Mrs Field came by her death as the result of manual strangulation, and that a man had been executed in relation to it.'

The jury at the inquest on Murphy held at the prison, returned a verdict of 'death through judicial execution properly carried out'. Commander R Tabitoe, the prison governor, said that the execution was performed humanely and without a hitch. Dr F J W Sass, the prison medical officer, said that death was instantaneous.

Police Killer Saved from Gallows, 1948

On St Valentine's Day, 14 February 1948, during the early evening, PC Nathaniel Edgar, was on plain-clothes duty, in Wade's Hill, Southgate following a spate of burglaries in the area. He stopped a man and questioned him. Three shots were heard and passers-by reported the sound of running footsteps along Broadlands Avenue. PC Edgar was found dying outside 112 Wade's Hill. Before he died, he managed to whisper the name of his assailant to colleagues. PC Edgar had also written the name of the man in his notebook along with his address and identity number. The name read 'Donald Thomas, 247 Cambridge Road, Enfield'.

Donald George Thomas was a twenty-three-year-old army deserter and had been on the wanted list since the previous October. He was not at the Enfield address but was later traced to a boarding house, run by Mrs Smeed, in Stockwell through the publication of a photograph of a married woman, Mrs Winkless, with whom he was having an affair. He was arrested in his room and the murder weapon, a Luger pistol was found under his pillow, which he had vainly tried to reach as the police burst into the room. He had also a large quantity of ammunition, a rubber cosh and a book, *Shooting to Live with the One-Hand Gun*. When arrested, Thomas remarked: 'You were lucky. I might as well be hanged for a sheep as a lamb.' He was tried, convicted of murder and sentenced to death. However, Thomas was uniquely reprieved because Parliament was testing abolition of the death penalty and the trial took place during the five-year suspension period.

Reasonable Doubt Saves Murderer & Mutilator, Finchley, 1949

In 1949, Donald Hume, a second-hand-car dealer, murdered his business associate Stanley Setty (a forty-six-year-old Iraqi, whose real name was Sulman Seti), who was also a petty criminal, by stabbing him with a Nazi SS dagger at 620b Finchley Road. He cut up the body and put it into three parcels which he weighted with bricks. Hume had a private pilot's licence. He flew a light aircraft over the English Channel and dropped the parcels into the sea. One parcel washed up at Burnham-on-Crouch, Essex, on 21 October and fingerprints from the hands in the package identified the victim as Setty, who had been reported missing from his home in Lancaster Gate since 4 October.

Scotland Yard's enquiries eventually led them to Hume, after they visited the United Services Flying Club at Elstree and found bloodstains in an Auster sports plane that had been hired by Hume on 5 October. He was charged with murder and, on 18 January

1950, appeared at the Old Bailey, before Mr Justice Lewis. He claimed to know nothing about the murder, but said he had agreed to dispose of the parcels for three crooks he named as Mac, Greeny and 'The Boy'. The jury acquitted him on grounds of reasonable doubt. He was, however, sentenced as an accessory to the crime and jailed for twelve years. He served eight of them, receiving the maximum remission for good behaviour, being released from Dartmoor in the spring of 1958.

After his release, Hume admitted that he had invented the crooks and had simply based his descriptions of them on detectives who had interviewed him. His confession was printed in four issues of the *Sunday Pictorial*, which was reputed to have paid him £2,000 for the story. Under English law he could not be tried again for the same crime, and with the proceeds made from his confession, he went to Switzerland, where he spent most of the money on high living. He returned to the United Kingdom to commit two armed robberies, on 2 August 1958, when he held up the Midland Bank at Brentford in Middlesex, getting away with over £1,000, and on 12 November at another Midland Bank on the Great West Road. This time he got away with just a handful of notes, having shot and seriously wounded the manager. He returned to Switzerland, where he murdered again, shooting fifty-year-old taxi driver Arthur Maagr, during an aborted bank robbery in Zurich in January 1959. He was soon captured and tried. Found guilty of murder, there being no death penalty in Switzerland, Hume was sentenced to life imprisonment with hard labour. In August 1976 the Swiss authorities judged him insane and returned him to Britain, where he was incarcerated in Broadmoor. In 1988, at the age of sixty-seven and considered low risk, he was moved to a hospital in West London.

Truly a mother-in-law from Hell, Hampstead, 1954

In 1954, the ground floor and first floor of 11 South Hill Park, Hampstead were occupied by the family of a Greek Cypriot named Stavros Christofi, who worked as a wine waiter in the West End at London's famous Café de Paris. Stavros lived with his German wife Hella and their three children. After about fifteen years of marriage, the family were joined in 1953 by Stavros's mother, Mrs Styllou Christoffi. Styllou Pantopiou Christofi was illiterate even in her native language. Unable or unwilling to learn either English or German, she had great difficulty communicating with her daughter-in-law, who became the object of her hatred and obsessive jealousy.

On the evening of 29 July 1954, while Stavros was at work and the children in bed, Mrs Christofi murdered Hella by hitting her on the head with a cast-iron ash plate, then strangling her. She then set about burning the body in the garden. John Young, a neighbour, witnessed Mrs Christofi poking what appeared to be a tailor's dummy. Some time later, Mrs Christofi stopped a passing motorist and in broken English told a pathetic tale. She said: 'Please come, fire burning, children sleeping.' When the police came, the blood and other evidence in the kitchen told an entirely different story. There is no doubt that Mrs Christofi was a horrible woman to have as a mother-in-law. In 1925, while two fellow villagers had held open the mouth of her own mother-in-law, Mrs Christofi had rammed a blazing torch down her throat, killing her. On that occasion she was acquitted. However, this time she was not so lucky. She was tried at the Central Criminal Court before Mr Justice Devlin. She refused to plead insanity and was found to be sane by three doctors. On 28 October she was found guilty of murder. Mrs Christofi was hanged at Holloway by Albert Pierrepoint on 13 December 1954. By coincidence, the last two women to be hanged in Britain committed murder in the same street just nine months apart. A stone's throw away from the Christofi house, Ruth Ellis shot David Blakeley in April 1955 (see Chapter 8).

Ronald Marwood, Holloway, 1958

On 14 December 1958, in the early days of the 'Teddy Boy' era, Ronald Henry Marwood, a twenty-five-year-old scaffolder, was celebrating his first wedding anniversary. He lived with his twenty-five-year-old wife, Rosalie, in Huntingdon Street, Islington. Trouble flared up between two rival gangs, the Angel Mob and the Finsbury Park Lot, outside Eugene Gray's Dancing Academy at 133 Seven Sisters Road near that part of Holloway known as Nag's Head. Amongst other weapons, knives, bottles and knuckledusters were used. When matters got out of hand the police intervened. While 6 feet 5 inches, twenty-three-year-old police constable Raymond Henry Summers was arresting his best friend,

WEST END FINAL

Evening Standard

41,956   WEDNESDAY, MAY 6, 1959   ● ● 2½d.

MARWOOD MUST DIE —BUTLER DECIDES

'Most anxious consideration . . . but the law must take its course'

EXECUTION ON FRIDAY FOR KNIFING P-c

There will be no reprieve for Ronald Henry Marwood, the 25-year-old Islington scaffolder, who knifed to death P-c Raymond Summers in a gang fight outside a Holloway dance hall. Marwood will be hanged on Friday.

RONALD MARWOOD
There were two petitions.

Mr. Butler, the Home Secretary, announced his decision today in a letter to Mr. Albert Evans, Socialist MP for South West Islington.

Mr. Evans presented to the Home Secretary a reprieve petition signed by 150 MPs—six Tories, one Liberal and 143 Socialists.

In his letter, Mr. Butler said:

Dear Evans, I have given the most careful and anxious consideration to the representations which you and others have made to me about the case of Ronald Marwood.

'REGRETFULLY'

Marwood was convicted after a very full trial of the capital murder of a police officer acting in the execution of his duty; and an appeal against his conviction was dismissed.

I have examined the case in the light of all the available information and all the relevant circumstances; and I have failed to discover a sufficient ground to justify me in recommending Her Majesty to exercise the Royal prerogative of mercy.

I have regretfully come to the conclusion, therefore,

'I shall try to see him again,' says his 20-year-old wife

Evening Standard Reporter

Twenty-year-old Mrs. Rosalie Marwood said at her mother's home near Regent's Park this morning: "I shall try to see my husband again although he told the prison chaplain that he did not want any more visitors if his reprieve was turned down."

She was asleep when a special messenger arrived with a letter from the Home Secretary, Mr R. A. Butler, saying there would be no reprieve.

Her mother, Mrs. A. Stephenson, said: "My daughter took the news very badly and a little later Father Thomas Hulhoven called to comfort her.

Very brave

Father Hulhoven and the Rev. W. J. Jenner, vicar of St. Silas's, Islington, were the organisers of a petition for Marwood's reprieve.

Mrs. Marwood was taken out by a friend for a drive this afternoon. On the way they stopped to pick up Marwood's father, Harry, and his mother, Sally, at their terraced house a few streets away from Pentonville Prison.

P-c SUMMERS
Stabbed outside dance hall.

Kettners has no music and is not luxurious . . . but the Food & Wines are superb, whether served in the restaurant or the small banqueting rooms.

Kettners RESTAURANT
romilly street, soho, w.1.

MRS. ROSALIE MARWOOD
"She read the letter slowly."

SNOW

Snow two and a half inches deep fell in the Shetland Isles this morning.

Small-ads. received by 9 p.m. can appear next day. Ring FLEet Street 5000

'Worst since Judas'

Says John Osborne

By The Londoner

Wearing a powder-blue sweater, playwright John Osborne today gave me his views on the slating by the critics and the booing by sections of the audience of his first musical, The World of Paul Slickey.

Appropriately, he stood with his back to the wall of the cluttered sitting-room in his Chelsea house. Eyeing a pile of newspapers, he said: "I have had the worst notices since Judas Iscariot.

"It was what I expected, this was premeditated. There's no question of complaining. But not one daily paper critic has the intellectual equipment to assess my work or that of any other intelligent playwright.

"There was an insistent note of hysteria throughout. I would hate to have good notices from those people."

The booing

What of the booing? "It's a distinction to be booed by some people," said Osborne. "It is the only way some frustrated little people have of shooting off their ears. I thought the cheers just about balanced the boos."

Osborne did not attend the first night party after the show. Why? "I felt too tired," he said, "and it would have been a great circus. I came home and fell asleep in half an hour."

I asked whether he thinks the show will flop. "There is no way of telling" said Osborne.

Some day he may write a good one. Osborne is 29.

Milton Shulman writes on
PAGE SEVEN

Britain protests

Britain is protesting against the firing of shots by an Icelandic gunboat near the trawler Arctic Royal.

A note is being handed to the Icelandic Government today.

Trains delayed

An engine failure near Crewe made main-line trains from Euston up to 90 minutes late this morning.

● Page Twelve, Col. Three

As the terms of your petition have been published in the Press I am sending them a copy of this reply on the morning of Wednesday May 6.

Extra police were detailed today for duty at Pentonville Prison when Marwood is hanged.

They will be there as a precaution against possible demonstrations.

4 KILLED AS PLANE FALLS IN STREET

A Dove aircraft crashed on a parked van in North Road, Cardiff, near Maindy Stadium, this afternoon. Police said four bodies had been recovered and there might be more.

The aircraft, operated by Lec Refrigeration Co., of Bognor Regis, exploded and burst into flames.

Mr. Peter Gough, director of a nearby garage, said: "There was no engine noise, just a thump. We ran out and just as we got to the airplane there was an explosion. I think it was the van's petrol tank going up.

Road blocked

"The van, which was empty, was completely destroyed. Fortunately there was little traffic about because of early closing."

The crash blocked the North Road, main route to North Wales. The road is a mile from Cardiff's city centre and seven miles from Cardiff Airport.

An official of Lec Refrigeration Company Limited said the company was operating an aircraft at the Cardiff Ideal Home Exhibition at Maindy Stadium.

It was a "flying showroom" and aboard Mr. and Mrs. Burchell, two representatives and Lec directors.

£55,000 PICASSO

Sotheby's today . . . as a nude by Picasso, painted in 1905, is sold for £55,000—a world record.—See The Londoner's Diary: Page FOUR.

The Shah at Guildhall

The Shah of Persia received the welcome of the City of London at Guildhall this afternoon on the second day of his State visit.—Page THIRTEEN.

Ernie's £50 winners

The 250 winning numbers in the May Premium Bonds draw are on PAGE FOURTEEN.

Mr. K for U.S.A.?

United States State Department officials will probably invite Mr. Krushchev to visit America soon.— Page ELEVEN.

Radio and Television

programmes—Page 9

Fleeing prisoner crashes in lorry

A lorry with an escaped prisoner at the wheel forced a policeman who signalled it to stop to leap for safety at Porthampton, near Tewkesbury, Gloucestershire, today.

The lorry crashed into a police car blocking the road and recaptured 28-year-old Brian Julian, who had escaped from Gloucester prison.

WEATHER—Mainly fine.—See Page 13.

Front page news . . . Evening Standard

Marwood was said to have pulled a 10-inch knife out and stabbed him in the back. The policeman died of his injuries.

Eleven youths were charged with brawling but Marwood, who denied any involvement, was released. However, he attracted attention to himself when he disappeared. The killing of a policeman was a very serious matter indeed and Marwood's unexplained absence from home threw suspicion his way. He hid out with some friends in Chalk Farm. The police issued a picture, on 3 January 1959 and he gave himself up on 27 January, when he walked into a police station and allegedly admitted, 'I did stab the copper that night.' This claim was later denied by Marwood, who insisted the police 'put down things' he did not say. At his trial, which took place at the Old Bailey in March 1959, Marwood said he heard Police Constable Summers telling the brawlers to break it up and he struck out at the officer, intending to push him away. He also said he did not know he had a knife in his hand. It transpired that on the night of the murder during his anniversary celebrations Marwood visited various pubs where he consumed ten pints of brown ale. The defence claimed there was no evidence connecting the accused man with the fatal blow but if, in the excitement of the fight he did stab the constable, whilst his brain was clouded with drink, then the verdict should be one of manslaughter. On 19 March, Ronald Marwood was convicted of the capital murder of a policeman and became the first person to be sentenced to death under the section of the Homicide Act of 1957 that protected police officers and warders. He was hanged at Pentonville on Friday 8 May 1959. There is a widely held belief, in pockets of North London communities, that Marwood was in fact entirely innocent of the killing of PC Summers. The alleged real killer being one of Marwood's close associates, who later achieved national fame and indeed celebrity status more than two decades after Marwood was hanged.

CHAPTER 8

The Tragic Case of Ruth Ellis
Hampstead, 1955

As Ruth fired the last bullet it missed Blakely, hit the pavement, ricocheted and struck the hand of a passer by.

Of all UK murder cases throughout the centuries, few have attracted the same degree of attention, scrutiny and indeed controversy as that of the tragic story of Ruth Ellis and the killing of her lover David Blakely. What singles the case out above all others, is that Ruth Ellis was the last woman to be hanged in Britain. Some less generous-spirited commentators have said that had this 'ice-cool' murderess not been a young woman with undoubted physical attractions, then the case would not have warranted so much media attention, nor indeed prompted the degree of public indignation following her conviction for murder and subsequent execution. Indeed, they do have a point, particularly when one considers other murder cases around that time where the perpetrators have been women; and also Ellis's executioner, Albert Pierrepoint's comments in his autobiography on the same subject, quoted later in this chapter. Indeed, there was no such outcry a few months prior to Ellis's execution in December 1954, when Mrs Styllou Christofi was hanged at Holloway, for murdering her daughter-in-law (see Chapter 1). Ellis and Christofi were the last two women to be hanged in Britain and, co-incidentally, committed their crimes nine months apart, just a matter of a few dozen yards apart in the same street in Hampstead.

That Ruth Ellis killed David Blakely was never in doubt and when the jury reached their verdict, Mr Justice Havers passed the only sentence available to him. She died at the end of a hangman's rope, in the execution shed at Holloway Prison, on 13 July 1955, the fifth woman to be hanged there since 1903. No men were ever hanged at Holloway Prison. Sadly, no posthumous reprieve, pardon or lessening of the severity of her crime could ever alter that fact, but campaigners have worked tirelessly for over half a century to see her crime reduced to manslaughter. The most recent call to overturn her murder conviction, considered by appeal court judges Lord Justice Kay, Mr Justice Silber and Mr Justice Leveson in September 2003, was not successful. Lord Justice Kay delivered the judgement on 8 December 2003, dismissing the appeal as 'without merit'. When one considers the facts of the case and the law as it stood at the time, one can hardly disagree with their Lordships' judgement.

A little after 9.00pm on Easter Sunday 10 April 1955, a bleached, platinum blonde woman wearing a grey two-piece suit and green sweater was seen peering through the window of the saloon bar of the *Magdala Tavern*, in South Hill Park, a short distance from Hampstead Heath railway station. A customer, Alan Thompson (who within just a few short minutes was to play a significant part in events), noticed her from where he was sitting in the saloon bar. Having looked through the window, the young woman retreated and waited in the doorway of a newsagent's shop next door. Ruth Ellis had made her way to South Hill Park earlier that evening from her home at 44 Egerton Gardens, Kensington. As she waited she put on her black-rimmed spectacles.

Inside the *Magdala Tavern* were twenty-five-year-old racing driver David Blakely and his friend, thirty-year-old Mayfair car salesman (Bertram) Clive Gunnell. Blakely cashed a cheque for £5 with the landlord, Mr Colson. The two men stayed in the bar for about ten or fifteen minutes, according to Gunnell. They had a couple of drinks and Blakely purchased three flagons of beer before they left the pub to go back to the party they had left in nearby Tanza Road.

As they left the *Magdala Tavern*, Blakely carrying one flagon of beer, Gunnell carrying two, Blakely went to open the driver's door of his Vanguard, which was parked immediately outside the doorway, facing downhill with the driver's door nearest the kerb. As Blakely stood by the car, feeling for his keys in his pocket, two men standing nearby noticed a young blonde woman as she stepped out from the doorway of Hanshaw's newsagents. She called out, 'David'. Blakely did not answer, neither did he acknowledge that she was even there, but carried on searching his pockets for his keys while still cradling the beer he had bought just a few moments before.

The Magdala Tavern, *with the former newsagents to the right, South Hill Park, Hampstead.* Paul T Langley Welch

As the woman drew up close to Blakely she swiftly put her hand into her handbag and drew out a .38 Smith & Wesson revolver. She did not utter another word but raised the gun and pointed it directly at Blakely. He turned and ran towards the front of the Vanguard to seek cover, but as he did so, Ellis fired two shots into his back in quick succession. Blakely slumped into the side of the car, smearing it with blood, and reached out to his friend, who was standing rigid with astonishment, and called out, 'Clive'. She then fired another shot and, as the bullet entered his body, Blakely contorted in agony and fell face down, with his head at the point where the *Magdala Tavern* met Hanshaw's, his left cheek on the ground. Ellis walked up to the now-motionless body and pumped more shots into it. She emptied the revolver, until all six rounds had been fired and the empty gun clicked as she continued to pull the trigger. Fewer than two hundred yards away, in the garden of Wentworth Place, a little over a 140 years before, another lover, the poet John Keats, wrote what became arguably his most famous poem, *Ode to a Nightingale.*

At least four of the six bullets tore through Blakely's body, causing considerable damage to his vital organs as well as massive shock and haemorrhaging. As Ruth fired the last bullet, it missed Blakely, hit the pavement, ricocheted and struck the hand of a passer by, fifty-three-year-old Mrs Gladys Kensington Yule, who was walking to the *Magdala Tavern* with her husband. The bullet passed through her left hand at the base of her thumb before fragmenting and hitting the beige tiled wall of the pub. Witnesses said Ellis did not appear to notice Mrs Yule's cry of pain. The motionless body of David Blakely lay on the pavement surrounded by a mixture of blood, frothing beer and broken glass. Ellis, still holding the gun, said quite calmly to Clive Gunnell, who was holding his dying friend, 'Now go and call the police, Clive.' She stood trembling, with her back against the pub wall.

Inside the *Magdala Tavern* was the person who had seen Ruth Ellis peering through the window just a short while before. He was an off-duty policeman, Police Constable 389, Alan Thompson, of L Division of the Metropolitan Police. He was having a quiet drink while he waited for his girlfriend to arrive when someone rushed unto the bar shouting, 'A bloke's been shot outside.' Police Constable Thompson went outside to investigate. Ruth Ellis was standing with her back to the pub wall clutching the revolver in her right hand and still pointing it towards David Blakely. Police Constable Thompson calmly walked up to her, took the gun from her hand and put it in his pocket. As he did so, Ruth Ellis said to him, 'Will you call the police?' He replied, 'I am the police.' 'Will you please arrest me?' she said. Ruth then received the first of three cautions delivered to her that night.

Officers were quick to arrive from nearby Hampstead Police Station. An ambulance was soon at the scene and David Blakely was accompanied by Clive Gunnell to New End Hospital, where he was pronounced dead on arrival. Mrs Yule's husband could not wait for an ambulance but summoned a taxi, whose driver agreed to take them to the hospital only on condition that she hold her blood-dripping hand out of the cab window to avoid staining the interior of his vehicle.

Accompanied by several burly policemen, Ruth Ellis (who stood just 5 feet 2 inches tall) was taken to Hampstead Police Station in nearby Rosslyn Hill. There she made a statement that was witnessed by three senior CID officers from S Division: Detective Superintendent Leonard Crawford, Detective Chief Inspector

Leslie Davies and Detective Inspector Peter Gill. The statement read:

> I have been cautioned that I am not obliged to say anything unless I wish to do so and that anything I do say will be taken down in writing and may be given in evidence. I understand what has been said. I am guilty. I'm rather confused. About two years ago I met David Blakely when I was manageress at the *Little Club*, Knightsbridge. My flat was above that. I'd known him for about a fortnight when he started to live with me, and has done so continuously until last year when he went away to Le Mans for about three weeks' motor racing. He came back to me and remained living with me until Good Friday morning. He left me about 10.00am and promised to be back by 8.00pm to take me out. I waited until 9.30 and he had not phoned although he had always done so in the past. I was rather worried at this stage as he had had trouble with his racing car and had been drinking. I rang some friends of his named Findlater at Hampstead, but they told me he was not there, although David had told me he was visiting them. I was speaking to Mr Findlater and I asked if David was alright. He laughed and said, 'Oh yes, he's alright.' I did not believe he was not there and I took a taxi to Hampstead where I saw David's car outside Findlater's flat, at 28 Tanza Road. I then telephoned from nearby and when my voice was recognized they hung up on me. I went to the flat and continually rang the doorbell but they would not answer. I became very furious and went to David's car which was still standing there and pushed in three of the side windows. The noise I had made must have aroused the Findlaters as the police came along and spoke to me. Mr Findlater came out of his flat and the police also spoke to him. David did not come home on Saturday and at nine o'clock this morning, Sunday, I phoned the Findlaters again and Mr Findlater answered. I said to him, 'I hope you're having an enjoyable holiday' and was about to say because you have ruined mine and he banged down the receiver. I waited all today for David to phone but he did not do so. About eight o'clock this evening I put my son Andrea to bed. I then took a gun which I had hidden and put it in my handbag. This gun was given to me about three years ago in a club, by a man whose name I do not remember. It was security for money but I accepted it as a curiosity. I did not know it was loaded when it was given to me

but I knew next morning when I looked at it. When I put the gun in my bag I intended to find David and shoot him. I took a taxi to Tanza Road and as I arrived David's car drove away from the Findlater's address. I dismissed the taxi and walked back down the road to the nearest pub where I saw David's car outside. I waited outside until he came out with a friend I know as Clive. David went to his car door to open it. I was a little way away from him. He turned and saw me and then turned away from me and I took the gun from my bag and I shot him. He turned round and ran a few steps round the car. I thought I'd missed him so I fired again. He was still running and I fired the third shot. I don't remember firing any more but I must have done. I remember then he was lying on the footway and I was standing beside him. He was bleeding badly and it seemed ages before an ambulance came. I remember a man came up and I said, 'Will you call the police and an ambulance.' He said, 'I am a policeman.' I said, 'Please take this gun and arrest me.' This statement has been read over to me and it is true.

Signed
Ruth Ellis

Ruth Ellis was charged with murder at 12.30pm on Easter Monday, 11 April 1955. The following day, she made a brief appearance at Hampstead Magistrates' Court before being removed to Holloway Prison, where she became prisoner number 9656.

The woman we know best as Ruth Ellis was born on 9 October 1926, at 74 West Parade in the North Wales seaside resort of Rhyl. Her father, Arthur Hornby, was a musician who used the professional name, Arthur Neilson, and the name Neilson appeared on Ruth's birth certificate. Ruth's mother, Bertha, was half-French and half-Belgian. She came to England during World War One, after fleeing Liege to escape the Germans and worked in service until she met and married Arthur Hornby. Ruth was the third of six children and from an early age was myopic (near-sighted) and needed spectacles, although as she became more conscious of her appearance and adopted sophisticated tastes, she seldom wore them. However, on the night of Easter Sunday, 10 April 1955, in readiness for the onerous task she had set herself, Ruth put on her black-rimmed spectacles. She was normally too vain to wear them and did so only if it was absolutely necessary. On that night she clearly felt it was necessary

In 1933, Ruth's family moved to the South of England after Arthur Neilson found work with a band at Basingstoke in Hampshire. A few months later, he was out of work and Ruth's father's fortunes steadily declined. He found work as a porter in a mental hospital and, with his promising musical career seemingly over, he took to drink. His drinking habits grew worse and the family was subjected to the backlash of the frustrations of an irascible and morose failure. Her father was to be Ruth's first experience of many men who sought solace at the bottom of a glass of one form of alcohol or another. Arthur Neilson continued working as a porter until 1938, when at the beginning of the Second World War, he took a job as a caretaker at Reading in Berkshire. The family went with him. Ruth left school in 1941 and later that same year her father found work as a chauffeur in London. The job brought with it a two-bedroom flat and Ruth went to live there with her father. She found herself work in a munitions factory and then at a food-processing company. It was during this period that she began to bleach her dark brown hair with peroxide. She spent her leisure hours at dance halls, cinemas, cafes and drinking clubs, although she was still only sixteen-years-old. Furthermore, she was determined to enjoy herself, and nurtured hopes of improving her prospects and lifestyle by mixing with a 'better class' of people.

In March 1942, Ruth was taken ill with rheumatic fever and after her discharge from hospital she took the medical advice she was offered that dancing would help strengthen her body and aid recovery. As a result of her dancing, she found a job as a photographer's assistant at the Lyceum Ballroom in London's West End. It was there, at the age of seventeen, in late 1944, that she met and fell in love with a French-Canadian soldier. After a brief affair she became pregnant. Her lover promised many things but not unlike many similar wartime romances, all came to nothing. Not long after Ruth became pregnant, a bunch of red roses and a letter arrived at 19 Farmers Road, Camberwell, where Ruth was then living with her family. Her lover was on his way back to Canada where he had a wife and two children. Ruth would never see him again. Ruth gave birth to an illegitimate son on 15 September 1945. The child was born in a private nursing home at Gisland, deep in the Northumbrian countryside. She christened him Clare Andrea Neilson. Clare was his father's name. The boy, however, was usually called Andy. On her return to London, Ruth met with a mixed reception from her family. It was her elder sister, Muriel, to whom she turned to for support. Muriel could be relied on most and it was this much-loved sister who acted as surrogate mother to Andy in the years that followed.

In need of a job to support herself and her son, Ruth found work as a model at a camera club. She soon found herself posing nude while the camera club devotees snapped away, pointing lenses at Ruth's attractive form, seen through viewfinders of cameras often containing no film at all. As with many such clubs, both then and now, Ruth was being exploited by members of what amounted to little more than a pervert's paradise. Occasionally, after work, Ruth would be invited out by club members and taken to the numerous drinking clubs that proliferated the West End. It was in one such club that she met Morris Conley, a wealthy businessman and night-club owner. Ruth first came into contact with Conley (usually known as Maury or sometimes Morrie) at the *Court Club*, 54 Duke Street. Conley was impressed with Ruth and decided that she had the right personality, charm and air of authority to operate as a good club hostess. He offered her a job and Ruth joined six other hostesses. The pay was good. She also had a clothing allowance, free drinks and for Ruth, perhaps most importantly of all, she was able to mix with the 'better class' of people she yearned for. Ruth worked in various clubs owned by Conley over a nine-year period. Her advancement through his shady organisation had its price and Ruth found herself obliged to succumb to various sexual favours; and she often found herself at the brunt of Conley's abuse when he was drunk. As well as Conley, Ruth gave sexual favours to various clients and, early in 1950, she became pregnant by one of her regular customers. She had an abortion and returned to work almost immediately. Ruth began drinking heavily and in the summer of that year she was to meet a man who was to become a major influence in her life. However, characteristically for Ruth, once again, he would be the wrong sort of man.

One night in June 1950, Ruth was working at the *Court Club*. A customer by the name of George Ellis was very persistent in his attentions to her and kept pestering her to spend the evening with him. She had heard about him from the other hostesses who called him 'the mad dentist'. He was lavish with money and told outlandish stories about his exploits. Ruth had made other plans for the night and intended to go out partying. However, to get rid of

Ellis, she agreed to meet him later at another club owned by Conley, the *Hollywood*. She never turned up. The next day Ruth was mortified to discover that while Ellis was waiting for her outside the *Hollywood* he had made approaches to a woman who, unbeknown to him, was with some East End gangsters from Bethnal Green. One of them attacked George Ellis and slashed his face with a razor. He was rushed to hospital where he received emergency surgery at St Mary's Hospital, Paddington. When he made an appearance at the *Court Club*, his face stitched, Ruth felt sorry that she had persuaded him to meet her at the *Hollywood*, knowing full well she would not be turning up. She agreed to go to dinner with him. Chauffeur driven to George's golf club at Purley Downs, Ruth returned home with George to his house in Sanderstead, Surrey.

So began a whirlwind courtship. In George Ellis, Ruth might just have found the man who would give her that better lifestyle she had dreamed of. After all, divorcee George Johnson Ellis was a dentist. Musically talented, he held what was then something of a rarity, a private pilot's licence. He was also a hopeless alcoholic. He was born on 2 October 1909, in Manchester. He married and he and his wife Vera had two sons. The marriage was not happy. George drank heavily and his frequent bouts of drinking led to mood swings which all too often displayed his violent temper. One day, he returned home to Sanderstead to discover that his wife and children had left, taking with them the household furnishings. Afterwards, George Ellis spent an ever increasing time in bars and clubs until the night he met Ruth Neilson. George was very generous where Ruth was concerned and showered her with gifts. He took her on a three-month holiday to Cornwall, and on their return, Ruth took up residence at George's house in Sanderstead. George was very fond of gin and tonic and he was hitting the bottle heavily. The situation grew worse until George agreed to admit himself into Warlingham Park Hospital in Surrey, where he received treatment for alcoholism. Shortly after his release Ruth and George married at the Registry Office, Tonbridge, Kent, on 8 November 1950. George found work at a dental practice at Southampton early in 1951 and they moved to Hampshire. George remained sober for a time but after a few weeks he became a regular in the local pub and his drinking increased. Soon he and Ruth were arguing, both at home and in public and after one particularly violent confrontation, Ruth packed her bags and went to stay with her parents. Two days later she went back to George. It was about this time that Ruth, possibly as a result of her own heavy drinking, became paranoid and started to become very jealous. She convinced herself that not only was George drinking but when he was away from her he was womanising. The fights continued and George beat Ruth badly from time to time. She left him and returned to him on numerous occasions. The situation worsened and on more than one occasion the police had to be called. By May 1951 the dental practice that George had joined had had enough of him and he was asked to leave. George admitted himself to hospital once again, for detoxification. Ruth visited him often but her jealousy continued and she developed a phobia and convinced herself that George, whilst a patient himself, was having improper relations with the female staff and patients. During one particular visit she became so hysterical that she had to be physically restrained and sedated. The psychiatrist who was at that time looking after her husband, Dr T P Rees, prescribed drugs for Ruth and she remained under his care until the day she killed David Blakely.

On 2 October 1951, Ruth gave birth to a 7-pound baby girl at Dulwich Hospital. The baby was named Georgina. On the birth certificate, the father's address was given as 7 Herne Hill Road, Lambeth, Ruth's parent's residence. George was still in hospital in Warlingham. Shortly after Georgina was born, George took a job as school's dental officer and moved to Warrington in Cheshire. He filed a petition for divorce on the grounds of cruelty. Ruth was now in urgent need to find work. She turned to Maurice Conley who was delighted to see her. He gave her a job at what had been the *Court Club* but which had been renamed *Carroll's*. Refurbished, the club now included a restaurant, cabaret and dancing and stayed open until 3.00am. Conley arranged for Ruth to move into a block of flats owned by his wife, Hannah, Flat 4, Gilbert Court, Oxford Street. Ruth soon became a popular and favourite hostess at *Carroll's*. In December 1952, she became ill, and after treatment it was found she had developed an ectopic pregnancy. After an operation, she remained in hospital for two weeks and by April 1953 had returned to work. Business was good at *Carroll's* and Ruth's effervescent personality oiled the wheels with the customers and much to the approval of Maurice Conley, made them lose their money. Not long before Ruth moved on from *Carroll's* club, during the long hot summer of 1953, a new group of people started using the club; they raced cars for a living and based themselves at the *Steering Wheel Club*, situated across the road from the *Hyde Park Hotel*. They often came to *Carroll's* club during the afternoons. On one particular afternoon in September, Ruth had her first encounter there with David Blakely. She did not gain a very favourable impression of him and commented:

> He strolled in wearing an old coat and flannel trousers. He greeted the other lads in a condescending manner . . . I thought he was too hoity-toity by far.

She called him a 'pompous ass' after he behaved appallingly to the hostess.

In October 1953, Conley offered Ruth the job of managing one of the clubs he owned, the *Little Club*, situated at 27 Brompton Road, Knightsbridge. Unlike his larger clubs where there were many staff, the *Little Club* was a more intimate establishment. Ruth would run the club with three staff and she was given a two-bedroom flat above the club, £15 a week salary and £10 a week entertainment allowance. Already a member there, David Blakely was embarrassed when confronted by the new manageress at the *Little Club*, the woman who had ticked him off at *Carroll's*. He became one of Ruth's regular customers and the attraction that developed between them was to prove fatal to both parties.

David Blakely was born in a Sheffield nursing home called Oakdale, on 17 June 1929. He was the youngest of three sons and a daughter, of Dr John and Mrs Anne Blakely. His parents divorced in 1940 and his mother remarried in 1941, a successful businessman, millionaire and one of Britain's best known racing drivers, Humphrey Wyndham Cook. David was sent to boarding school in Shrewsbury where he demonstrated little attitude for academic achievement but a considerable one for motor cars and motor racing. After leaving school, he completed two years' mandatory National Service in the Army and afterwards his stepfather's influence found him work as a management trainee at the *Hyde Park Hotel*. Brown-eyed, with long, silky eyelashes, David Blakely, stood 5 feet 9 inches tall and weighed about 11 stone (154 pounds). He left school with the classic public school aura of self-confidence. Spoilt as a child, he was self-assured, arrogant, frivolous with money, prone to horseplay and when full of drink, prone to violence, as later was proved by his treatment of Ruth

Ellis; although where men were concerned, he would hide behind women's skirts to escape the trouble he had provoked.

As well as his salary from the *Hyde Park Hotel*, David received money from his stepfather and an allowance from his mother, which enabled him to maintain a second-hand sports car, an HRG, named after the designer H R Godfrey, bought for him as a twenty-first birthday present by his stepfather. He entered it in various races and gained experience as a racing driver. Dr John Blakely, his father, died suddenly in February 1952. David received £7,000 as his share of his father's estate. He formed a relationship with a regular customer at the *Hyde Park Hotel*, Miss Linda Dawson, the daughter of a wealthy industrialist from Huddersfield. This did not prevent David from having affairs with numerous other women, including an American model, a theatre usherette and Carole Findlater, the wife of his friend, Anthony, whom he had first met in 1951 when Ant, the pet name by which Findlater was usually known to his friends, was trying to sell an Alfa Romeo sports car. David was sacked from his position at the hotel, in October 1952, following an altercation with the banqueting manager, after which his mother took him away on a world cruise. On his return he joined a manufacturing company, Silicon Pistons, of Penn in Buckinghamshire, a company situated conveniently near the new family home. Although he had use of a flat attached to this house, David preferred to spend his time at his stepfather's London home at 28 Culross Street, Mayfair. A little over a month after David had first met Ruth Ellis, he became engaged to Linda Dawson and an announcement appeared in *The Times* on 11 November 1953. This event did not prevent him sleeping with Ruth at her flat above the *Little Club*. Ruth did have a number of regular clients that she still entertained from the old days, and this was often during the afternoons before the club opened. However, Ruth's affair with Blakely was driven by affection and not by money. If it had been, she would have been sorely disappointed because it was to Ruth that David turned to for money, whenever he was short, which was often.

The affair between Ruth and David continued and Ruth stated:

In December 1953 I had an abortion by him and he was very concerned about my welfare. Although he was engaged to another girl, he offered to marry me and he said it seemed unnecessary for me to get rid of the child, but I did not want

to take advantage of him. I was not really in love with him at
the time and it was quite unnecessary to marry me. I thought I
could get out of the mess quite easily. In fact, I did so with the
abortion.

At the beginning of 1954, George Ellis reappeared on the scene.
He visited Ruth at the *Little Club* and was pressing for their divorce
to become final. She was stalling for time in order to keep the
maintenance money he was paying. One problem was what should
be done with their three-year-old daughter Georgina. Ruth's living
conditions and lifestyle were not condusive to bringing up a little
girl. After considerable deliberation it was decided that George
should take the child back to Warrington to arrange adoption. This
finally occurred in May 1954.

Ruth first met Ant Findlater when David brought him to the
club, sometime around April 1954. When Carole Findlater organised a thirty-third birthday party for her husband, she telephoned
Ruth and invited her. Carole was curious to see what David's new
mistress was like. The Findlaters lived in a second-floor flat, at
29 Tanza Road, Hampstead. On meeting, the two women were
unimpressed with each other and there was very little commu-
nication between them.

In June 1954, David went to Le Mans to dive in the twenty-four-
hour race and returned in the middle of July. He sent Ruth two
postcards. It was during David's absence that Ruth, angry that her
lover had stayed away so long, had an affair with thirty-two-year-
old Desmond Cussen. Cussen was born in Surrey and had been
an RAF pilot during the Second World War, flying Lancaster
Bombers. After demobilisation in 1946 he studied for and became
an accountant. Afterwards, he was appointed a director of his
family's business, Cussens & Co, a wholesale and retail chain of
tobacconists with branches in London and Wales. He was a car
enthusiast although he never raced professionally himself. He
found companionship at the *Steering Wheel Club*. Cussens had met
Ruth at *Carroll's* club, long before David Blakely came on the scene
and he and Blakely had no liking for each other. On David's
return, she forgave him for leaving her for so long and, on 17 June
1954, David arrived late for his twenty-fifth birthday party,
organised by Ruth. He explained that he had been to the *Hyde
Park Hotel* to break off his engagement with Linda Dawson. He
asked Ruth to marry him.

David raced at Zandvoort in Holland in August 1954, in an MG owned by a friend and this time he invited Ruth to join him. She was pleased he had offered to take her but turned him down as she had to make arrangements concerning her son, Andy's education. Andy, then ten years old, was sent off to boarding school, his school fees and uniform paid for by Desmond Cussen.

For many months David had been occupying his spare time building a racing car he called 'the Emperor'. He paid Ant Findlater £10 a week to work on it. Building the car was a costly exercise and David's rapidly dwindling funds were being further eaten into. The money he made at the piston factory and the allowance his mother gave him was hardly covering his expenses. He asked Ruth if he could move in with her. She allowed him the privilege and also allowed him a 'slate' (account) at the club. Both of them began to drink heavily. In October, Ruth hosted he twenty-eighth birthday party at the club. Blakely sent her a telegram from Penn. Both parties were becoming jealous of the other. Ruth had found out about his affair with Carole Findlater and he was frequently violent towards her, often after he became jealous over events that occurred in the club bar – events that he referred to as 'tarting around'. Where Ruth Ellis was concerned Blakely was jealous and possessive when she was in the company of other men.

Towards the end of the year, takings at the *Little Club* had fallen from over £200 a week to less than eighty. Ruth had let David run up a bar bill that he could never repay. Whether of her own volition or whether she was asked to leave, Ruth left the *Little Club* in December 1954. Homeless and needing a place to stay for herself and Andy when he returned from boarding school for the Christmas break, she turned once again to Desmond Cussen, who allowed her to move in with him at his spacious flat, 20 Goodwood Court, Devonshire Street, Marylebone. David was furious that Ruth had moved in with Cussen but she placated him by telling him that by breaking away from the club life, she had taken her first step towards respectability, something he had been wanting her to do. She assured him that she would not sleep with Cussen and between 17 December 1954 and 5 February 1955, Ruth and David spent several nights at the *Rodney Hotel*, Kensington. She told Cussen that she was staying the night with girlfriends or visiting her daughter, Georgina, in Warrington. On Christmas Day 1954, Ruth hosted a party at Cussen's flat. Cussen was attending a business party elsewhere and did not return home until later that evening when the party was in full swing. David was there and he argued with Ruth because she had left her son sleeping in the flat while she and her guests had gone out clubbing. The usual nasty altercation took place and he accused her of sleeping with Cussen whilst she accused him of carrying on his affair with Carole Findlater. The drunken pair left the party and made their way to Tanza Road where they discovered the Findlaters were out. David let himself in and he and Ruth spent the night there. Cussen, concerned about Blakely's ability to drive in his drunken state, had followed them. He watched the house until about 9.00pm then returned home to his party guests and the still sleeping Andy at Goodwood Court, minus the hostess. On Boxing Day, Ruth returned to Cussen's flat and explained her absence by telling him that David had threatened to commit suicide if she didn't spend the night with him.

That same day, David raced *The Emperor* for the first time at Brand's Hatch, in the Kent Cup, in which he came second. By early in the New Year, Ruth had convinced herself that David was having an affair. She got Cussen to drive her to Penn. A little detective work ensued and Ruth saw David leaving the home of a good-looking married woman, older than himself, whose husband was away on business. She had a blazing row with him during a stay at the *Rodney Hotel* on 8 January, about this affair. He left for Penn and having not heard from him, Ruth sent David a telegram on the 10th which read:

Havent [sic] you got the guts to say goodbye to my face – Ruth.

David was disgruntled by this and afraid that Ruth might get some of her gangster friends to call on him, friends she had met through her contacts working in the shady clubs of Morris Conley, something she had threatened to do on several occasions. He mentioned his fears about this to Ant Findlater and told him he wanted to get away from Ruth for good and never see her again. However, by the 14 January, David and Ruth were back together again in the *Rodney Hotel* and on that day Ruth received her *decree nisi*, her divorce from George Ellis would be absolute in six weeks. The final obstacle would be removed and there was nothing to stop them marrying. Ruth continued to suspect that David was having an affair and got Desmond Cussen to drive her around. The ever faithful Desmond, inordinately fond of, if not infatuated with

Ruth, allowed herself to be treated like a lap dog. He also did his own spying and it was not long before he discovered that David and Ruth were meeting at the *Rodney Hotel*, he never mentioned the fact he knew about it to Ruth.

On 6 February, a major row took place in Cussen's flat while Desmond was away. David called his friends Ant Findlater and Clive Gunnell, claiming that Ruth had tried to stab him. When they arrived they found a drunken Ruth with a black eye, limping, and covered in bruises. David was also drunk, had a black eye and was limping. Ruth had David's car keys and she would not give them to him. She did not want him to leave and at one point she lay in front of Gunnell's car to prevent him leaving by that means. Eventually, after Ruth had sobered up, the three men left in Gunnell's car and Ruth returned to Goodwood Court. On Desmond's return, she had him drive her around looking for David. They went to the Findlater's flat, and then to the *Magdala Tavern*, a favourite for David and his friends. Another journey took them to Euston where Ruth tried to trace a woman David had mentioned during one of their ever increasing drunken brawls and onto Penn and Gerrards Cross where David's car was seen outside a pub. An altercation took place and David was in danger of being beaten by Desmond. He took off for London before any damage was done. That afternoon, Ruth received a bunch of red carnations. The accompanying card read:

Sorry darling, I love you, David.

When they met later that night, David explained his behaviour by saying he was jealous because she was staying in Desmond's flat. They agreed to look for somewhere to live of their own, providing they could borrow some money. Desmond lent them the money but Ruth kept him sweet by promising to visit him from time to time and she kept a spare set of keys to Desmond's flat. On 8 February 1955, Ruth took out a lease on a flat, at 44 Egerton Gardens, Kensington, a tall, red-brick building, consisting of furnished serviced rooms, managed by housekeeper Mrs Winstanley and situated near the Brompton Oratory. Ruth and David moved in as Mr and Mrs Ellis. On 22 February, there was another row about the woman in Penn and Ruth sustained a black eye and severe bruising. In early March Ruth, David and Desmond attended the British Racing Drivers' Club dinner and dance at the *Hyde Park Hotel*. She danced alternately with both of them. Ruth retired that night to Egerton Gardens and David joined her. The following morning, she asked him to leave and for the next week she spent her time with Desmond. Ruth had decided on a change of career and Desmond, as well as buying her a new set of clothes, was financing her in a modelling course. He drove her there each morning and picked her up after her lessons were over.

In March 1955, Ruth found that she was once again pregnant. The pregnancy resulted in a miscarriage during the last week of that month, after Blakely had once again been violent towards her and, as well as inflicting other injuries, he had punched her in the stomach. Ruth said:

> ... he only used to hit me with his fists and hands but I bruise easily, I was full of bruises on many occasions.

Exactly who was the father might have been is hard to determine.

David had entered *The Emperor* at a race meeting at Oulton Park, near Chester, due to take place on Saturday 2 April. On 31 March, David, Ruth and Ant drove to Cheshire and David and Ruth booked into a hotel as Mr and Mrs Blakely. Unfortunately, Blakely never got to drive *The Emperor* at the main meeting, as the car broke down during one of the practice laps. On the Saturday night, David and Ruth held a party at their hotel. Carole Findlater had joined her husband the previous night and she recalled that David and Ruth argued constantly, he blaming her for jinxing his car and she telling him:

> I'll stand so much from you David, you cannot go on walking over me forever.

To which Blakely replied:

> You'll stand it because you love me.

On her return to London on Sunday night, feeling ill, she was feverish and had a temperature of 104 degrees. On Monday, Desmond called to see her at Egerton Gardens and insisted she stay in bed while he went to pick Andy up from his boarding school for the Easter holidays. Ruth was rapidly growing tired of Blakely's abuse and his attitude towards their relationship was causing her a great deal of distress. Matters were soon to reach a climax.

Andy came to Egerton Gardens and slept on a camp bed in his mother's bedroom. David visited her late in the evening on both Monday and Tuesday, telling Ruth he had been attending to matters concerning *The Emperor*. On the Wednesday, he brought her a photograph of himself. It was a promotional photograph for the Bristol Motor Company's works team. He had been selected to race in the Le Mans twenty-four hour race on 9 June. On it he had written:

To Ruth with all my love, David.

In January, Ruth had started taking French lessons, paid for by Desmond Cussen. She wanted to surprise David with her linguistic skills, when they went to the race. On the Thursday they had arranged to go to the theatre but David was latte arriving at Egerton Gardens and instead they went to the cinema, where David kissed and caressed her and told her how much he loved her.

On Friday morning, Good Friday 8 April, David left Egerton Gardens at about 10.00am. He told Ruth he had a meeting with Ant to discuss matters concerning *The Emperor* and he had promised Ruth that he would not visit Ant in Tanza Road without telling her. Ruth did not trust Ant and she trusted Carole Findlater even less. Before he left, David and Ruth had made plans to take Andy out the following day. When, by 9.30pm, David had not returned to Egerton Gardens, she telephoned the Findlaters. The telephone was answere by their nineteen-year-old nanny. She said there was no one at home. She rang again later and spoke to Ant who told her that David was not there but she knew from his voice that that was not the case. She called Desmond who agreed to drive her to Tanza Road in his black Ford Zodiac saloon. On her arrival at No 29, Ruth rang the doorbell of the Findlaters' flat repeatedly and banged on the door. Nobody answered. David's dark-green Vauxhall Vanguard, registration OPH 615, was parked outside. It had originally been a van but David had partially converted it to a saloon, by removing the metal side panels and replacing them with windows, held in place by rubber strips. It was about 2.00am when someone in the house called the police, after Ruth, screaming and shouting abuse set about the car and pushed in several windows. Ant appeared on the doorstep in pyjamas and dressing gown and Ruth demanded to see David. At that point a police inspector arrived on the scene. He tried to persuade Ruth to go home but she told him:

I shall stay here all night until he has the guts to show his face!

No 39 Tanza Road, Hampstead. The Findlater's flat was at the top of the building.
Paul T Langley Welch

After making another attempt at persuading her to leave, and unwilling to interfere in a domestic situation, the inspector left the scene.

Ruth spent the entire night walking around the Vanguard and watching the Findlater's flat from various points. She had convinced herself that the Findlaters were deliberately coming between herself and David and that he must be having an affair. She suspected that this new rival might be the Findlaters' nanny. At about 8.00am, Ant and David cautiously emerged from the flat and drove off in the Vanguard. They did not notice Ruth watching them from a nearby doorway. Ruth returned home to Egerton Gardens and gave her son some money, before she sent him off alone to spend the day at the zoo.

Once again, Ruth persuaded Desmond to drive her to Hampstead. She went to the *Magdala Tavern* but he was not there. Later that evening, she was back outside the Findlaters' flat – where inside she could hear what sounded like a party going on. She convinced herself that Blakely was there and that the Findlaters' nanny was the subject of his amorous attentions. The next day, Easter Sunday, Blakeley's friend Clive Gunnell brought his record player to the Findlaters' flat and the assembled company prepared themselves for yet another session of music and partying over the holiday weekend. It was about 9.00pm that David and Clive decided to go to the *Magdala Tavern* for a drink and to get some beer and cigarettes. They drove to the pub in David's Vanguard. As they pulled away from outside 29 Tanza Road, Ruth Ellis was just arriving. She watched the car disappear and turned up outside the *Magdala Tavern* a few moments later. Less than fifteen minutes afterwards, David Blakely was lying dead outside, and shortly after that Ruth Ellis would be taken into custody and charged with his murder.

Following the removal of David Blakely's body from Hampstead's New End Hospital, it was taken to Hampstead Mortuary where a post-mortem examination was conducted by pathologist Dr Albert Charles Hunt. The injuries sustained were as follows: there was an entry wound above the left hip bone going through the skin and underlying fat and exiting immediately in front; another entry wound behind the left shoulder blade going through the chest, the left lung, the aorta and the wind pipe, the bullet was found lodged in the deep muscle to the right of the tongue; a third bullet entered through the lower part of the back, going through the intestines and the liver and ended up lodged in the ribs; there was also a shallow graze on the inner surface of the left arm, consistent with a fall resulting from the first bullet; his stomach contents showed that he had consumed four pints of beer.

The cause of death was shock and haemorrhaging as a result of gun shot wounds.

The trial of Ruth Ellis lasted a day and a half and began in the No 1 Court at the Old Bailey, on Monday 20 June 1955, before Mr Justice Havers. The prosecution was lead by Mr Christmas Humphreys, QC, Mr Griffith-Jones and Miss Southworth; and the defence lead by Mr Melford Stevenson, QC, with Sebag Shaw and Peter Rawlinson. Against the advice of her defence, who wanted to create an entirely different impression, Ruth appeared in court in a tailored black suit, with astrakhan collar and cuffs, over a white-satin blouse. Her freshly-bleached hair was neatly coiffured, after special permission had been given by the governor of Holloway, Dr Charity Taylor, and her face meticulously made up. Instead of giving the appearance of a vulnerable, confused woman, a victim of agonising circumstances, the impression she created resembled 'a hard-faced tart'. Indicted for the murder of David Blakely, on the advice of her defence, she pleaded not guilty. However, the decisive question asked by prosecution counsel Mr Christmas Humphreys, QC, sealed Ruth's fate. He asked Ruth:

> Mrs Ellis, when you fired that revolver at close range into the body of David Blakely, what did you intend to do?

Ruth's reply was:

> It is obvious that when I shot him I intended to kill him.

Mr Melford Stevenson, QC, in his opening address to the jury, told them that he was going to invite them to reduce this charge of killing, from murder to manslaughter on the grounds of provocation. He also said:

> The fact stands out like a beacon that this young man became an absolute necessity to this young woman. However brutally he behaved, and however much he spent of her money on various entertainments of his own, and however much he consorted with other people, he ultimately came back to her, and always she forgave him. She found herself in something like an emotional

prison guarded by this young man, from where there seemed to be no escape.

Mr Justice Havers could not allow a change to the crime for which Ruth was being tried and gave a lengthy explanation of his reasons. Havers warned the jury that in view of the evidence it was not possible to return a verdict of manslaughter. His Lordship said there was not:

> ... sufficient material, even on a view of the evidence most favourable to the accused, to support a verdict of manslaughter on the grounds of provocation.

Melford Stevenson then said, in view of the judge's ruling, it would not be appropriate for him to say anything more to the jury. In his summing up Mr Justice Havers reminded the jury once again that it was not open to them to bring a verdict of manslaughter. His concluding remark seemed to seal Ruth Ellis's fate:

> I am bound to tell you that even if you accept the full evidence it does not seem to that it establishes any sort of defence to the charge of murder.

The jury of ten men and two women retired at 11.52am and returned after twenty-three minutes at 12.15pm. They found Ruth Ellis guilty of wilful murder. As Mr Justice Havers donned the black cap, Ruth Ellis stood, unmoving. After sentence had been pronounced, she replied:

> Than you.

There was an enormous public outcry at the verdict. The death penalty abolitionists vehemently expressed their opposition to the hanging of Ruth Ellis. The anti-abolitionists also had their day, one in particular. If Ruth had wanted to choose a more vindictive passer-by to injure on the night she shot David Blakely, she would have been hard pressed to find one. The bank official's wife, Mrs Gladys Kensington Yule, who was injured by a ricocheting bullet when she was walking down South Hill Park from Parliament Hill with her husband, was herself in a highly tense state and she and her husband were on their way to the *Magdala Tavern* for a recuperative drink. Just two days before, on Good Friday, Mrs Yule's son from a previous marriage had committed suicide. At the trial, Mrs Yule stated that as she and her husband walked down Parliament Hill towards the *Magdala Tavern*, she saw a woman and two men in the vicinity of the public house. She heard five shots, two before Blakely fell and two after he fell and the last shot hit her. Gladys Yule was a staunch anti-abolitionist. She wrote in the *Evening Standard*, on 11 July 1955:

> Don't let us turn Ruth Ellis into a national heroine. I stood petrified and watched her kill David Blakely in cold blood, even putting two further bullets into him as he lay bleeding to death on the ground. What right had Ruth Ellis to be jealous of Blakely, jealous to the point of killing? Even if there had been another woman she had another lover during the same period, that had been proved in evidence. What proof have we that the allegations against Blakely are true? He is dead and cannot defend himself. It is therefore distasteful and cruel to start a smear campaign against the boy, to try to justify a dastardly murder. Those hysterical people getting petitions for a reprieve and those rushing to sign them. Do they realize Ruth Ellis shot Blakely to the danger of the public? She might easily have killed an innocent passer-by, a complete stranger. As it is, I have a partly-crippled right hand for life, for which there is no compensation. If Ruth Ellis is reprieved, we may have other vindictive and jealous young women shooting their boyfriends in public and probably innocent blood on their hands. Crime passionel indeed! What if other countries would let her off from her just punishment? When has Britain followed the lead of others? Let us remain a law abiding country, where citizens can live and walk abroad in peace and safety.
>
> Mrs Gladys K Yule,
> Parliament Hill,
> Hampstead.

Ruth decided against an appeal. There would have been no point as there were no legal grounds on which to base one. Despite considerable public and press pressure and a petition containing 50,000 signatures requesting clemency, the Home Secretary, Major Gwilym Lloyd George, could find no grounds for reprieve, and on Monday 11 July, Ruth received notice of this fact from the prison governor. Thirty-five members of London County Council delivered their plea for clemency to the House of Commons on Tuesday 12 July, but to no avail. On the Tuesday evening, the eve of the execution, a large crowd gathered outside the gates of Holloway Prison. Some broke through a police cordon and banged on the prison gates, shouting for Ruth to pray with them.

As the crowds gathered outside Holloway prison, inside preparations were being made for the hanging. Ruth had been weighed so the correct length of rope could be calculated. This was not an exact licence but to an experienced executioner such as Albert Pierrepoint (who hanged over 400 men and women over a twenty-five year period), it provided sufficient information to ensure that death was swift. The gallows had been tested that afternoon using a sandbag weighing exactly the same as Ruth. It had been left overnight on the rope to remove any stretch. At about 7.00am, Albert Pierrepoint and his assistant Royston Ricard had reset the trap and coiled the rope up above it so as to leave the leather-covered noose dangling at chest height.

The *Daily Mirror*, 13 July 1955, described the morning of execution:

THE WOMAN WHO HANGS THIS MORNING
By Cassandra

It's a fine day for hay-making. A fine day for fishing. A fine day for lolling in the sunshine. And if you feel that way – and I mourn to say that millions of you do – it's a fine day for a hanging.

If you read this before nine o'clock this morning, the last dreadful and obscene preparations for hanging Ruth Ellis will be moving up to their fierce and sickening climax. The public hangman and his assistant will have been slipped into the prison at about four o'clock yesterday afternoon.

There from what is grotesquely called 'some vantage point' and unobserved by Ruth Ellis, they will have spied upon her when she was at exercise 'to form an impression of the physique of the prisoner'.

A bag of sand will have been filled to the same weight as the condemned woman and it will have been left hanging overnight to stretch the rope.

Our Guilt ...

If you read this at nine o'clock then-short of a miracle – you and I and every man and woman in the land with a head to think, and a heart to feel will, in full responsibility blot this woman out.

The hands that place the white hood over her head will not be our hands. But the guilt – and guilt there is in all this abominable business – will belong to us as much as to the wretched executioner paid and trained to do the job in accordance with the savage public will.

If you read this after nine o'clock, the murderess Ruth Ellis, will have gone. The one thing that brings stature and dignity to mankind and raises above the beasts of the field will have been denied her – pity and the hope of ultimate redemption.

The medical officer will go to the pit under the trap door to see life is extinct. Then, in the barbarous wickedness of this ceremony, rejected by nearly all civilised peoples, the body will be left to hang for one hour.

Dregs of Shame

If you read these words of mine at mid-day the grave will have been dug while there are no prisoners around and the Chaplain will have read the burial service after he and all of us have come so freshly from disobeying the Sixth Commandment which says thou shalt not kill.

The secrecy of it all shows that if compassion is not in us then at least we retain the dregs of shame. The medieval notice of execution will have been posted on the prison gates and the usual squalid handful of louts and rubbernecks who attend these legalised killings will have had their own private obscene delights.

Two Royal Commissions have protected against these horrible events. Every Home Secretary in recent years has testified to the agonies of his task, and the revulsion he has felt towards his duty. None has ever claimed that executions prevent murder.

Yet they go on and still Parliament has neither the resolve nor the commitment, nor the wit, nor the decency to put an end to these atrocious affairs.

When I write about capital punishment, as I have often done, I get some praise and usually more abuse. In this case I have been reviled as being 'a sucker for a pretty face'.

Well, I am a sucker for a pretty face. And I am a sucker for all human faces because I hope I am a sucker for all humanity, good or bad. But I prefer the face not to be lolling because of a judicially broken neck.

Yes, it is a fine day.

Oscar Wilde, when he was in Reading Gaol, spoke of 'that little tent of blue which prisoners call the sky'.

The tent of blue should be dark and sad at the thing we have done this day.

Cassandra was the pen name of Sir William Connor.

Holloway Prison, where Ruth Ellis was executed. Author's collection

On the morning of her execution, Wednesday 13 July 1955, Ruth rose at 6.30am. In her cell was the photograph of David's grave she had requested some weeks before. She wrote a letter to David's mother and one to her solicitor. In preparation for her execution, Ruth was given a large brandy by the prison doctor and she knelt in prayer before a crucifix on the cell wall (a remnant of the stay there of Mrs Christofi, excuted the previous December), as she was served with communion by the prison chaplain. At a little after one minute to nine, Albert Pierrpoint entered the condemned cell. He pinioned Ruth's hands behind her back with his special calf-leather strap. He then led her the fifteen feet to the gallows and positioned her on the trap. While he drew a white cotton hood over her head, his assistant pinioned her legs with another leather strap. Pierrepoint then placed the noose over her head which secured the hood. He adjusted the rope's suspension point about an inch in front of her lower left jaw, then quickly removed the safety pin from the base of the lever, and immediately pushed the lever away from him to release the trap, which opened and through it Ruth plummeted. The whole process from Ruth leaving the condemned cell, took no more than ten or twelve seconds. While all this was taking place, around a thousand people stood quietly outside the prison. The prison doctor examined the body in the gallows pit to show life was extinct before the execution chamber was locked and the body of Ruth Ellis was left to hang for the customary one hour. At 9.18am the execution notice was posted on the prison gates and shortly afterwards the crowd began to disperse. Ruth Ellis became the last woman to be hanged in Great Britain. As well as being the fifth woman to be hanged at Holloway prison, she was also the sixteenth woman to be hanged in the whole of Great Britain during the twentieth century.

Albert Pierrepoint commented:

> When I left Holloway after the execution of Ruth Ellis, the prison was almost besieged by a storming mob. I needed police protection to get me through. I knew that I would have walked out of Strangeways [where a forty-year-old harridan had just been reprieved] a week earlier into an empty street. At Euston Station a crowd of newspapermen were awaiting me. I shielded my face from the cameras as I ran for my train. One young reporter jogged alongside me asking, 'How did it feel to hang a woman, Mr Pierrepoint?' I did not answer. But I could have asked: 'Why weren't you waiting to ask me that question last year, sonny? Wasn't Mrs Christofi a woman too?'

At 10.00am Ruth's body was taken down and removed to the autopsy room situated adjacent to the gallows pit. There, pathologist Dr Keith Simpson, performed an autopsy on the body, and he, as well as noting that the stomach contents had 'small residue, and odour of brandy', mentioned that the 'deceased was a healthy subject at the time of death'. The cause of death was given as 'injuries to the central nervous system consequent upon judicial hanging'. Shortly after this further abomination of Ruth Elli's body had been carried out, at about noon, she was buried within the precincts of Holloway prison.

In 1970, the rebuilding of Holloway prison required that the bodies of the five women executed at Holloway be moved. Along with those of the Islington baby-farmers, Mrs Amelia Sach and Mrs Annie Walters, executed in 1903; Mrs Edith Thompson, who arranged for her lover to murder her husband Percy and was found guilty of murder along with her lover, Frederick Bywaters, executed 1923; and Mrs Styllou Christofi, who murdered her daughter-in-law, Hella, executed 1954; Ruth Ellis was exhumed. The other executed women were buried in unmarked graves at

Brookwood cemetery in Surrey. Ruth's son Andy, then aged twenty-six, received permission to have his mother's body reburied where he chose and he originally selected a churchyard in Penn, Buckinghamshire, where David Blakely lies buried. However, permission was not granted, so Ruth was buried four miles away at St Mary's parish church, Amersham, Buckinghamshire, where a headstone was erected bearing the inscription:

RUTH HORNBY
1926–1955

The headstone was smashed to pieces some years later by Ruth's son Andre during a fit of depression, shortly before his own death.

The story of Ruth Ellis and David Blakely has continued to arouse considerable public curiosity. There is so much that remains unexplained about this tragic case: a story of love, uncontrolled passion, violence, jealousy and hatred.

Why Dr T P Rees, the psychiatrist under whose care Ruth Ellis remained, was not called to give evidence at her trial is puzzling. The fact that if she was suffering from the effects of legally prescribed sedatives, combined with alcohol, at the time she fired the gun that killed David Blakely, might have put an entirely different slant on the trial's outcome. When she was examined by psychiatrists before her trial, they decided she was sane. The question remains: was she sane at the time she shot David Blakely?

Did Ruth intend to kill herself with that last bullet she fired into the pavement, which damaged the hand of Gladys Yule? Perhaps she did, but bottled out at the last moment. Perhaps that is why she offered no resistance to her arrest and accepted fate so calmly in the end accepting that the death sentence passed on her was simply a means of assisting her suicide. It has been suggested that Ruth was suffering from post-miscarriage depression at the time of the shooting, following the miscarriage she suffered about ten days previously. It has also been suggested that Ruth was mentally ill, suffering from battered wives' syndrome and post-traumatic stress disorder, a condition that was not recognised until the 1980s.

Ruth Ellis could not have fired such a weapon as she did without being familiar with how it worked. Various reports claim that two different sources verified that Desmond Cussen had taken her for target practice and shown her how to use the gun. In her initial statement to the police, she said she had taken a taxi to Hampstead on the night she shot David Blakely. No taxi driver ever gave evidence to verify this fact. In December 1973, details of an alleged statement made to her lawyers on the day before her execution were published in the British press. It revealed that another jealous lover of Ruth's had given her the gun and driven her to Hampstead on the night of the murder. The lover was supposedly Desmond Cussen. Duncan Webb stated in the *People* that Ruth had made a pact with the man who supplied the gun and drove her to Hampstead, not to reveal his name, provided he safeguard the future of her son. Desmond paid for Andy's schooling. He attended a boarding school in Surrey, St Michael's. However, Desmond Cussen, having sold his interest in the family business, emigrated in 1964. In June 1977, British television journalist Peter Williams interviewed Cussen in Australia. He denied that he had supplied Ruth with the murder weapon and that he had driven her to Hampstead on the night of the murder. Desmond Cussen died in Perth, Australia, on 8 May 1991, from complications resulting from a fall on 24 April. Ironically, he died of pneumonia and organ failure, following fracture-dislocation of the neck. He was sixty-eight-years old.

George Ellis comitted suicide in the summer of 1958. He had recently lost his job and went to Jersey where he booked into *La Chalet Hotel* at Corbiere. On Saturday 2 August, he killed himself by looping a rope round the sides of his bedhead and then around his neck. He suffered death by strangulation, the old form of hanging. Tragically, in 1982, Andre (Andy), Ruth's son, also committed suicide at his bedsit, 21 Sale Place, Bayswater, by taking a cocktail of alcohol and drugs.

Today, outside the *Magdala Tavern*, on the beige tiled walls beneath one of the windows, the holes from the fragmented bullet which had struck Mrs Gladys Yule can still be seen today. Plaques have occasionally marked the spot where the murder occurred but have soon disappeared, unscrewed from the wall, either by souvenir hunters or outraged local residents.

CHAPTER 9

Death of a Playwright
Islington, 1967

It became increasingly, and all too painfully clear to Halliwell that Orton's success was leaving his own pitiful efforts in the shade.

In the 1960s, what had once been the village of Isleden had evolved through several centuries to become Islington. For the most part, with only a handful of exceptions, Islington's many fine terraced Georgian houses and squares had become run down and many of them had been divided into flats and bedsits. The Borough's gentrification was yet to begin. The largely elegant streets we see in today's Islington were, in the 1950s and 1960s, drab and sometimes even dilapidated.

On Wednesday 9 August 1967, at about 11.40am, a chauffeur-driven car arrived outside 25 Noel Road, a typical Georgian Islington terraced house, which had been converted into flats. The car had been booked to take thirty-four-year-old playwright Joe Orton, to Twickenham Studios, where he was to discuss a film script for *Up Against It*. The driver got out of the car, went through the front door of No 25 and walked up the stairs to Flat 4 on the second floor. He knocked on the door but there was no reply and he couldn't hear anyone moving around. He went downstairs and checked with his office and was told to try again. After two or three more attempts at knocking on the door, he decided to look through the letterbox. Having done so, he noticed the light was on in the hall and in the room beyond and he could just see the head of a bald man from the nose upwards. The man appeared to be lying motionless on the floor. The chauffeur knew the man was not Mr Orton as he had driven him twice before. He went downstairs, concerned that something was seriously amiss and the police were summoned.

No 25 Noel Road, Islington. Paul T Langley Welch

When officers broke into the flat – a cramped affair, just a studio with kitchen and bathroom – they found the naked body of the flat's owner, forty-one-year-old Kenneth Halliwell. There were splashes of blood on his chest, head and hands. Nearby on a divan bed was his flatmate and lover, Joe Orton, wearing only a pyjama jacket. Orton had severe head injuries inflicted by nine hammer blows to the skull. A bloodstained hammer was lying on his chest on the counterpane that covered his body. Orton's blood and brain matter had been spattered on both the wall and ceiling.

On the desk in the room in which they died, Halliwell had left a note placed on top of a red leather binder that held Orton's diary. It read:

If you read this diary all will be explained.

K H

PS. Especially the latter part

Kenneth Halliwell was brought up in a large semi-detached house in Bebington, Wirral. His father was a chartered accountant. In September 1937, the month Kenneth started at Wirral Grammar School, his mother suffered a horrific death after being stung in the mouth by a wasp. Kenneth had been close to his mum, who had pampered him, but his father virtually ignored him. Halliwell tried all sorts of ruses to get his father's attention, including running away from home, but the man remained indifferent. Halliwell excelled at school, where his teachers said he would have no trouble getting into Oxford or Cambridge, but he wanted to be an actor.

One morning, Kenneth came down to the kitchen and found his father's body. Charles Halliwell had gassed himself. Kenneth turned the gas oven off and, after shaving and making himself a cup of tea, he went to report his father's suicide to the neighbours. The money his father left gave Halliwell a degree of financial security that would eventually see him through the Royal Academy of Dramatic Art (RADA) and enable him to purchase his own home in London.

John Kingsley Orton (Joe Orton) was brought up in Leicester in a working-class household. He first met Halliwell when they were both students at RADA in 1951. Halliwell was seven years older than Orton, and prematurely bald. Soon after they met, Orton moved into Halliwell's flat. They lived together from that point on until the day they died. After graduating from RADA, Orton found work as an assistant stage manager, then occasional employment as a jobbing actor. Halliwell's acting career never really took off. Orton was heavily influenced by Halliwell's apparent sophistication and intellect, and Halliwell took the easily influenced Orton under his wing. By the late 1950s they had all but abandoned any thoughts of acting and had decided on a literary career.

In 1959, Halliwell purchased the studio flat at 25 Noel Road, that from 1960 would serve as a base to enable them to write. Collectively, their output was prolific, and Orton eventually developed a unique style far removed from the pretentious scribblings of Halliwell. Once this partnership had been established, the support that each gave the other was to reach fruition in Orton's success as a dramatist. This close relationship was cemented during the period when homosexuality was still a crime.

Often bored with their lack of success at getting their work published, and to anaesthetise themselves from the sometimes tedious jobs they were obliged to take, they made mischief to amuse themselves. In 1962, Orton and Halliwell were arraigned at Old Street magistrates' court for stealing seventy-two books from Islington and Hampstead libraries, and wilfully damaging a number of them. The allegations included the removal of 1,653 plates from art books (many of which adorned the walls of the flat, forming part of Halliwell's extensive collages) and adapting the designs of various book jackets (sometimes with hilarious results, although the magistrates did not see it that way). Orton also had a penchant for writing false (and often very crude) blurbs. Among his favourite targets were the Gollancz editions of Dorothy L Sayers's Lord Peter Wimsey stories, which had blank yellow flaps. In one particular Sayers book, *Clouds of Witness*, he wrote:

> When Little Betty Macdree says that she has been interfered with, her mother at first laughs. It is only something that the kiddy had picked up off television. But when sorting through the laundry, Mrs Macdree discovers that a new pair of knickers are missing she thinks again. On being questioned, Betty bursts into tears. Mrs Macdree takes her to the police station and to everyone's surprise the little girl identifies P.C. Brenda Coolidge as her attacker. Brenda, a new recruit, denies the charge. A search is made of the Women's Police Barracks. What is found there is a seven-inch phallus and a pair of knickers of the kind used by Betty. All looks black for kindly P.C. Coolidge ... What

can she do? This is one of the most enthralling stories ever written by Miss Sayers.

It is the only one in which the murder weapon is concealed, not for reasons of fear but for reasons of decency!

READ THIS BEHIND CLOSED DOORS. And have a good shit while you are reading!

The total value of the damage to the library books was estimated at £450. They were each given a prison sentence of six months; then first taken to Wormwood Scrubbs and later separated, serving their time in different open prisons, Orton in HM Prison Eastchurch and Halliwell in HM Prison Ford Arundel. In his diary Orton wrote:

I was locked in my cell for twenty-three hours a day. I used to have half-an-hour's exercise in the morning and half an hour in the afternoon. Now this didn't worry me so much, but it worried a lot of other people. I used to read a lot.

On their release, the two resumed writing. Everything Joe Orton might have hoped for regarding the launch of his career as a successful playwright came about in 1963 when his work began to be taken seriously. Orton's originality as a dramatist was his uncanny ability to take taboo subjects and thoroughly offensive characters and make them palatable. Through humour, he skilfully guided his audience around previously unthinkable territory. *Entertaining Mr Sloane*, opened at the New Arts Theatre on 6 May 1964 and transferred to the Wyndham's Theatre in the West End on 29 June, before moving on to the Queen's Theatre on 6 October; and *Loot* was produced soon afterwards. Orton's success attracted considerable media attention and started him on a meteoric rise that placed him at the forefront of the New Wave theatre world of the swinging sixties. He was much in demand at social gatherings. At first Halliwell basked in Orton's success and joined in with it, but gradually the pair grew apart and as Orton's escalating lack of dependency on his long-term lover became all to apparent, Halliwell's jealousy and paranoia began to surface.

It became increasingly, and all too painfully clear to Halliwell that Orton's success was leaving his own pitiful efforts in the shade. It became evident that he would never be able to match the raw talent that Orton had honed to become one of the leading lights of the theatre world. In the homosexual scene in which Orton and Halliwell had circulated almost exclusively until recently, there had been no problem with Halliwell's place in Orton's life. But the more sober establishment found it more difficult to accept Halliwell. He gave the impression of a man with more pretensions than talent. Too wooden as an actor, and with his writing skills never quite reaching the mark, the only part of his life he seemed to have developed into anything approaching an acceptable art form was collage. The studio flat in which the couple lived was covered from floor to ceiling in Halliwell's collages. He attached great significance to his efforts in this field and once wrote to Peggy Ramsay, Orton's literary agent, to ask her opinion about them. John Lahr mentions this in his biography of Orton, *Prick Up Your Ears*. Halliwell wrote:

> I should like your opinion of my collage murals. Does my real talent if any lie in this direction etc? For instance, the woman who came to interview J for the *Evening Standard* this afternoon spent her time admiring my murals and saying did they cost a terrific lot of money and how professional they were, etc. This has happened before with all sorts of people.

Halliwell lacked the self-assurance to try to promote himself and advance his efforts in this field, but Orton encouraged him, and, in 1967, arranged an exhibition of fifteen pictures in Chelsea. A few were bought by Orton's associates but the general public showed no interest whatsoever.

Unlike Joe Orton, who enjoyed a highly varied sex life with a large number of sexual partners, Ken Halliwell was by comparison not only far less promiscuous but might almost be regarded as being sexually retarded. Joe used to tease Ken about his lack of success in pulling both men and boys and poked fun at his less than adventurous approach to all things sexual. Not only were Ken's meagre artistic efforts being overshadowed, which caused him no small degree of anxiety but he was also failing miserably in the most intimate part of his life. Halliwell was very self-conscious about his baldness and kept his hat on everywhere he went, including the theatre. In an attempt to help him overcome this, Orton bought Halliwell a wig out of the money he made from *Entertaining Mr Sloane*.

Halliwell's bouts of depression grew worse, becoming deeper and more frequent. The diaries kept by Orton, which span the relatively short period from December 1966 to August 1967, chronicle not only his literary successes, culminating in an *Evening*

Standard Drama Award, but also gave a candid account of his sex life, both with Halliwell and numerous casual men, often describing exploits in the most unusual circumstances and unlikeliest of places. He also mentions Halliwell's black moods, which were becoming more frequent, his violent outbursts and his rapid decline into self-doubt. The entry for Monday 1 May 1967 reads:

> Kenneth H. had a long talk about our relationship. He threatens, or keeps saying he will commit suicide. He says 'You'll learn then, won't you?' And 'What will you be without me?' We talked and talked until I was exhausted. Going round in circles. Later I went out and bought some haddock for the dinner tonight.

In the entry for Friday 5 May, Orton comments:

> When I got back home, Kenneth H. was in such a rage. He'd written in large letters on the wall 'JOE ORTON IS A SPINE-LESS TWAT'. He sulked for a while and then came round. He'd been to the doctor's and got 400 valium tablets. Later we took two each and had an amazing sexual session

On Wednesday 12 July Orton wrote:

> Spent the whole morning typing up *What the Butler Saw*. Kenneth is reading the second half of the play. He suggested one or two cuts. I shall take his advice. The play is long enough for me to cut anything that isn't a good line or necessary for the understanding of the play. He said he watched a programme last night in which Alastair Sim starred. Kenneth says that Sim would be ideal for Dr Rance. Agree with him. And Arthur Lowe as Dr Prentice. Kenneth also says that we should offer Mrs Prentice to Coral Browne. She would be rather good – though I doubt whether she'd accept. In the afternoon we went to the Palace Theatre with Sheila Ballantine and Kenneth Cranham to see *The Desert Song*, the old musical revived. It was a touring version which has been brought into the Palace because the modern American musical *110 in the Shade* flopped so rapidly. It's difficult to judge *The Desert Song* on this production. It was clearly written for great stars of the old type. Very funny. We all laughed at the ridiculous lines – though v. discretely because most of the audience (of old Ladies) were taking it seriously and enjoying it. Kenneth Halliwell said that a lot of it reminded him

of my writing. Not surprising really since my writing is a deliberate satire on bad theatre . . .

Then on Monday 17 July Orton's diary entry reads:

Kenneth v. irritating today. Weather hot again. Blue skies. Kenneth's nerves are on edge. Hay fever. He had a row this morning. Trembling with rage. About my nastiness when I said, 'Are you going to stand in front of the mirror all day?' He said, 'I've been washing your fucking underpants! That's why I've been at the sink!'

He shouted it out loudly and I said, 'Please, don't let the whole neighbourhood know you're a queen.' 'You know I have hay fever and you deliberately get on my nerves,' he said. 'I'm going out today,' I said, 'I can't stand much more of it.' 'Go out then,' he said, 'I don't want you in here.' I went to Boots for the enlargements of the holiday snaps. They'd merely duplicated them, not enlarged them. So I had to take them back. Long face from Kenneth. 'I should've taken them myself,' he said 'and why did you pay for them?' I took *What the Butler Saw* to Peggy. She looked at the title and said, 'Oh! It's just like the title of an old farce!'

The situation continued to deteriorate at home, but in his professional life further success was on the horizon. The diary entry for Sunday 23 July reads:

Yesterday morning Peggy rang me. Quite early. She'd read *What the Butler Saw* in a hotel room in York late on Thursday night. 'People must've thought I was mad,' she said. 'I simply had hysterics. It's the very best thing you've done so far.'

Orton made his last diary entry on Tuesday 1 August:

Said goodbye to Kenneth this morning. He seemed odd. On the spur of the moment I asked him if he wanted to come home to Leicester with me. He looked surprised and said, 'No.'

Throughout the pages of his journal Orton meticulously catalogued his day-to-day existence in a frank and open manner. His sexual exploits and feelings towards his friends, associates and acquaintances are all made clear. Orton's obvious fondness for Halliwell is apparent, as is his deep concern for Kenneth's mental health and their deteriorating relationship. Halliwell had easy access to these diaries and as he read them it must have become apparent to him that as his partner's rise continued, Orton was slipping away from him. It seems Halliwell was not prepared to let that happen. To prevent Orton leaving, Halliwell took a hammer and killed him as he rested in his bed. So ended the life of one of the most gifted and finest post-war English playwrights.

At the inquest, held before Deputy Coroner for St Pancras, Dr John Burton, evidence was given by Halliwell's doctor, Dr Douglas Ismay. The doctor said that Halliwell had made a previous suicide attempt seven years before, and had spoken to him about a holiday he had taken in Morocco with Orton earlier in 1967. Halliwell told Dr Ismay that while on holiday he had taken large quantities of hashish and had been eating it. Dr Ismay had arranged for Halliwell to see a psychiatrist.

Pathologist Professor Francis Camps, said:

I doubt that he knew he was being hit. There is nothing to suggest any sort of defence.

Having inflicted horrific injuries on Orton, Halliwell took a massive overdose of barbiturates. He emptied the twenty-two capsules of Nembutal into a bucket and mixed it with a tin of grapefruit juice, which speeded the powerful drug into his system and caused death very quickly. Professor Camps said:

From the fact that there was more of the drug in his liver blood than in his arms he died quite suddenly and did not simply become unconscious.

When the police broke into the flat, Halliwell's body was cold but Orton's, although life by then was extinct, was still quite warm. Douglas Orton identified his brother and Orton's literary agent Margaret (Peggy) Ramsay, identified Halliwell. Dr Burton recorded the jury's verdict that Mr Orton, aged thirty-four, was murdered by Mr Halliwell, aged forty-one, who then took his own life.

From 1967, the term 'Ortonesque' became part of the British vocabulary, a recognised description of 'macabre outrageousness'. Kenneth Halliwell's funeral took place at Enfield Crematorium on 17 August. It was attended by Peggy Ramsay and three of Halliwell's relations. Joe Orton's funeral took place at the West Chapel, Golders Green Crematorium, the following day. The funeral was arranged by Peggy Ramsay and Peter Willes, of Rediffusion's

Drama Department. It was a subdued gathering, attended by Orton family members and the cast of *Loot*. As Orton's coffin, draped in a maroon pall and covered in red roses, was carried into the chapel, a tape recording of the Beatles' *A Day in the Life*, from their album *Sergeant Pepper's Lonely Hearts Club Band* was played; it was Orton's favourite song. Donald Pleasance read his own poem, *Hilarium Memorium J.O.* Then Orton's friend Harold Pinter spoke a few lines and as the coffin slid away through the bronze doors, and the chapel emptied to the sound of Debussy's *Clair de Lune*. In the arcade, seventy wreaths had been laid out. A card on an iron stand bore the inscription 'Floral tributes for Mr Joe Orton'.

At Halliwell's funeral, one of his relatives proposed that his ashes be mixed with Orton's. Peggy Ramsay suggested this to Joe's brother, Douglas. He agreed, but added:

As long as nobody hears about it in Leicester.

The ashes were mixed together and buried in the Garden of Remembrance at Golders Green Crematorium.

CHAPTER 10

The 1960s and into the Millennium

Joe Meek, Holloway, 1967

Legendary homosexual record producer Joe Meek (Robert George Meek) was born in 1929, at Newent in Gloucestershire. After his stint of national service as a radar technician, he was briefly a television engineer, before becoming a recording engineer at IBC

A present-day view of 304 Holloway Road. The plaque above the shop sign was unveiled in March 2007, it reads: Joe Meek, Record Producer, 'The Telstar Man', 1929–1967, Pioneer of Sound Recording Technology, Lived Worked and Died Here. Author's collection

Studios, before going to work for the independent record producer, Landsdowne, where he engineered some of Lonnie Donegan's early hits. He began to write music and decided to branch out on his own. Meek is acknowledged as one of the world's first and most imaginative independent record producers. He built his own studio in a rented flat above Shentons travel goods and handbag shop at 304 Holloway Road, where he wrote and produced possibly his most notable work, *Telstar* (1962) for The Tornadoes, which has the distinction of being the first No 1 record by a British group in the USA. He was obsessed with the late Buddy Holly – and the occult. Meek had bouts of paranoia, which may have been fuelled by his drug taking. During a period fraught with self-doubt and financial uncertainty for Meek, he committed murder. On the morning of 3 February 1967, the eighth anniversary of Buddy Holly's death, Meek killed his landlady, Mrs Violet Shenton, firing a shotgun, before turning the gun on himself.

John Hilton, Golders Green, 1978

Wealthy diamond merchant, fifty-five-year-old Leo Grunhut, was ambushed by two men armed with a sawn-off shotgun in Limes Avenue, Golders Green, at 6.50pm on 28 February 1978. He was carrying almost £300,000 worth of precious stones and as he tried to flee, was shot in the back. As Mr Grunhut fell to the floor he was shot again. The two assailants grabbed their booty and fled in a white Vauxhall Victor. A blood trail at the scene suggested that one of the robbers had also been injured. Severely wounded Mr Grunhut died of his injuries at Hampstead's Royal Free Hospital, three weeks later. For over twelve years the identity of the killers remained a mystery. Then in December 1990 sixty-one-year-old John Hilton, a known villain, was captured on a concealed video camera during a jewel robbery in Piccadilly and subsequently arrested. Whilst on remand at Brixton Prison, Hilton was interviewed at his own request by Flying Squad officers. He confessed to every crime he had committed including the murder of Leo Grunhut. In shooting Mr Grunhut he had accidentally shot his accomplice Ian Roberts in the thigh and he had died as a result of massive blood loss. Hilton buried Roberts in a shallow grave on a railway siding at Stone near Dartford, Kent. He took police to locate Robert's remains on 26 February 1991.

On 9 September 1991, Hilton appeared at the Old Bailey before the Recorder of London, Judge Lawrence Verney. He pleaded guilty and told the jury:

> I want to come to terms with my conscience before I die. The history of armed robbery is littered with bodies. If Roberts had shot me in that incident then I have no doubt he would have acted afterwards in exactly the same way.

Hilton was sentenced to two life terms of imprisonment, with the recommendation that he serve at least thirty years.

Dennis Nilsen, Muswell Hill and Cricklewood, 1978–83

During the first week in February 1983, Dyno-rod, a drain cleaning company, was called to Cranley Gardens, Muswell Hill, to attend to blocked drains. When an inspection cover adjacent to No 23 was lifted, pieces of rotting flesh were clogging the pipes. No 23 Cranley Gardens was owned by an Indian woman who lived in New Delhi. The house was divided into flats and bedsits, managed by estate agents in Golders Green. The top floor flat had been occupied since 1981 by thirty-seven-year-old Dennis Nilsen, a mild mannered civil servant, who had formerly served in the army as a cook and on his discharge had briefly joined the police force. Once it had been established that the body parts were human, the police paid Nilsen a visit. When asked if he knew anything about the human body parts he enthusiastically poured out a horror story of how he had killed three men in his flat, dismembered them and boiled their heads in a pan on the kitchen stove. He had flushed pieces of flesh down the lavatory, which over a period of time had resulted in the drains becoming blocked. Body parts were found in black dustbin bags and three severed heads were found in a wardrobe. Nilsen admitted that at his previous home at 195 Melrose Avenue, Cricklewood, where he lived in the ground floor flat from 1976 to 1981, he had committed another twelve murders, the first being on the last day of 1978.

Nilsen often picked up men for casual sex. It transpired that in fifteen cases he could not bear the thought of being left alone, so he had 'killed for company', strangling his victims, often leaving them seated in the chair, presumably until the stench of decomposition urged him to dispose of their bodies. Most of Nilsen's victims were drifters. Some of them were identified as Malcolm Barlow, Martyn Duffey, John Howlett, Kenneth Ockenden, Steve Sinclair and Billy Sutherland.

Nilsen's trial began in the No 1 Court at the Old Bailey on 24 October 1983. At its conclusion on Thursday 3 November the jury took twenty-four hours to find him guilty. He was sentenced to life imprisonment with a recommendation that he serve at least twenty-five years. On Thursday 9 November 2006, the London *Evening Standard* were able to reveal the name of Nilsen's first victim, as a result of a letter they had received from his prison cell. Nilsen disclosed he had picked up fourteen-year-old Stephen Holmes, in a Cricklewood pub in December 1978 and, fearing he might leave him alone again, had killed him.

Patrick Folan, Holloway, 1981

In June 1999, a body found buried in a shallow grave beneath the concrete foundations of the modern extension of the Royal Northern Hospital, in Tollington Way, Upper Holloway, was later identified as that of Mrs Michelle Folan, who had disappeared some eighteen years previously, in October 1981. Michelle Folan, aged twenty-four and her twenty-six-year-old husband, Patrick, had been seen arguing in the *Half Moon*, a public house situated in Holloway Road, opposite the main building of the hospital, on the night she is believed to have last been alive. Demolition men, clearing the site of the extension to build a housing development, found Mrs Folan's fully clothed remains encased in concrete. Her head was shrouded with a plastic bag and the rope garrotte used to strangle her was still twisted around her neck.

Folan, a bricklayer by trade, had been working as a labourer on the building site when his wife disappeared. Michelle Folan's disappearance had baffled police, who had questioned her husband and reopened the case several times, having at one point dug up the patio in Folan's garden, although no charges were brought against Folan. With the help of relatives, including Mrs Folan's mother, Folan brought up the couple's two children at their Upper Holloway home in Bovington Close. Martin and Nicola Folan were aged three and sixteen months respectively, at the time of their mother's disappearance. It emerged that Michelle Folan had begun divorce proceedings against her husband, after two years of marriage, only days before she disappeared. Folan admitted that he had been violent towards his wife but maintained that she had run off, always trying to change the subject whenever the matter came up at family gatherings.

Folan was tried at the Old Bailey, where one witness remembered him as the quiet Irish bricklayer who helped to concrete the foundations of the hospital. Another witness, a close friend of Michelle Folan told the court, 'I thought she was being emotionally and physically tortured by him.' William Boyce, prosecuting, said, 'The body was concealed in a shallow grave dug in a place the person knew would soon be covered with a concrete floor. The person must have had inside knowledge of what was about to happen to the site.' Despite his continued denial, Folan was found guilty of his wife's murder and given a life sentence on 7 December 2001. In November 2006, Folan's case was reviewed at the Royal Courts of Justice. Mr Justice Jack ruled Folan must serve a tariff of at least fifteen years before being considered for parole and only then, if he can persuade the parole board that he poses no danger to the public could be released on a perpetual life sentence, subject to recall to gaol if he breaks his licence in any way.

Donald Mackay, Archway, 1989

In 1989, Donald MacKay murdered a twenty-six-year-old prostitute, Ann Petherick, who was last seen alive on 2 January. Following a visit to Mackay's Archway flat for sex on 17 February, by another prostitute, Rosemarie Saunders, police were called in. Mackay had tied Miss Saunders up and abused her in such a bestial fashion that she brought charges against him. In relation to that incident, Mackay was eventually convicted of 'threats to kill, assault with intent to commit buggery, indecent assault and assault occasioning actual bodily harm.' When police went to Mackay's flat on 19 February they found Ann Petherick's decomposing body in a bin bag. No exact cause of death could be established due to the amount of decay. Mackay had killed before. In 1984, he was found guilty of manslaughter after killing a man with a sword. Found guilty of murder at the Old Bailey in December 1989, he was sentenced to life, with a minimum tariff of twenty-years. In January 2007, an appeal to have his sentence cut was dismissed. He was told that the twenty-year tariff does not mean that he will automatically be released in 2009. Only if he can convince the Parole Board he is no longer a danger to the public, will he be released on a perpetual 'life licence', which would see him returned to prison for the slightest offence.

The Bodies in the Car Murders, Holloway, 1990

Michael Shorey, born in Barbados, became known as the Bodies in the Car Killer. On the morning of Monday 23 July 1990, passers by noticed two young women, apparently asleep in the front passenger seat and the back seat of a parked car, a gold Toyota Corolla, in Spears Road, Holloway. Concern was raised when workers at the various factories in the street noticed that neither appeared to be breathing. The police were called. Both women were dead. The car belonged to one of the victims, Patricia Morrison, aged twenty-eight, who with the other victim Elaine Forsyth aged thirty-one, shared a flat in Grenville Road, situated off Hornsey Road, Holloway. They also worked together at an estate agents.

Post-mortem examinations of the bodies showed that death must have occurred about thirty-six hours previously, on Saturday 21 July, and that both victims had been strangled. Pathologist Dr Vensa Djorovic, said Patricia had been approached from the front and strangled with a handbag strap, which was still around her neck when her body was discovered. Elaine had been attacked from behind and strangled with a curtain tie back chord, found in their flat. Neither had been sexually assaulted. Both women were badly bruised, suggesting they had attempted to fight off their attacker. Scotland Yard's Detective Superintendent Geoff Parratt, who headed the inquiry, concluded that the killer had put the bodies into the car and driven it to Spears Road.

An examination of the women's flat showed that they had been killed there. There were bloodstains on the walls and a carpet had been removed from the hall. Neighbours reported hearing sounds of screaming and fighting coming from the flat on Saturday evening but believed it to be a domestic row between the two girls. They had also heard bumping sounds, which was probably the killer taking the bodies down the stairs. Various reports came in of the car being seen being driven along Junction Road, Upper Holloway, during the rush hour on Monday morning, in a slow and erratic manner.

A detailed description of the driver was given. He was a young black man with long, permed hair. Police were approached by a former boyfriend of Elaine Forsyth, thirty-four-year-old accounts clerk, Michael Shorey. He fitted the description perfectly. He denied harming the two women. His former record of violence suggested things might be otherwise but after being questioned he was released. Shorey had given the missing length of carpet, wrapped in plastic to a friend to look after. When he heard about the murders, the friend contacted police. The carpet had blood and saliva from both murder victims.

Shorey was arrested and charged with double murder. Michael Shorey's trial began at the Old Bailey on 11 June 1991. Although some of the evidence was circumstantial, a pair of trainers worn by Shorey clinched the prosecution's case, when it was revealed they had traces of blood on them from both the murdered women. Found guilty of murder, Michael Shorey was jailed for life on 3 July 1991.

Anthony John Hardy, Camden Town, 2002

On 20 January 2002, police were called to a council flat in Royal College Street, Camden Town, after neighbours complained that fifty-year-old Anthony Hardy had been seen pouring battery acid through his neighbour's letterbox and writing obscenities on the door. Hardy was arrested and handcuffed. The police officers noticed that a bedroom door was locked. He claimed that the room was let to a lodger and he didn't have the key. The key was found in his possesion and when the door was opened there on the bed was a dead woman completely naked. Hardy was arrested on suspicion of murder.

The dead woman was thirty-eight-year-old prostitute and crack cocaine addict Sally Rose White. Although she had sustained cuts to her head and there were bite marks and bruising on her body, a post-mortem examination concluded that she had died of a heart attack; and death was attributed to natural causes. Hardy was charged with criminal damage for the other offences and examined by psychiatrists. When questioned about the dead woman he said he had drunk six litres of cider and a bottle of wine that day and had suffered an alcoholic blackout and had no knowledge of how the woman came to be in his flat.

On 30 December 2002, a vagrant was looking for discarded food in the bins behind the *College Arms*, in Royal College Street, when he found a bag containing human remains. Police later found eight more bags containing body parts, identified as coming from two different women who had both been killed within the previous few days. The hands and heads were never found. During their search police found a clear blood trail which led them to a block of flats and to Hardy's door. He was not at home. When they gained access, police found a hacksaw, an electric jigsaw covered in blood and a woman's torso wrapped in bin liners.

A nationwide search for Hardy was launched. Next day he was caught on CCTV at University College Hospital where had had gone to get drugs to treat his diabetes. It was not until 2 January that he was seen again at Great Ormond Street Hospital where he was arrested at 9.00pm.

Newspaper reports referred to Hardy as the Camden Ripper. The body parts were identified as belonging to Elizabeth Selina Valad, aged twenty-nine, identified by the serial numbers on her breast implants; and Brigitte MacClennan, aged thirty-four, identified by DNA testing. Both women were prostitutes with crack cocaine habits. On 6 January 2003, Hardy appeared at Hendon Magistrates' Court charged with all three murders. Initially Hardy claimed that he had not intended to kill anyone and that the women had died because of 'excessive force in the course of otherwise consensual but extreme sexual activity'. At his trial at the Old Bailey in November 2003 Hardy pleaded guilty to all three murders. On 23 November 2003 he was given three life sentences.

Dennis Ciantar, Holloway, 2004

Thirty-four-year-old, knife-carrying, unemployed crack-cocaine addict Dennis Ciantar was jailed for life on Monday 19 July 2004 for the cowardly lunchtime murder of bricklayer Gavin McGrath, also aged thirty-four. The murder took place on 14 September 2003, following a petty argument over queue jumping in the fast food outlet McDonald's, in Seven Sisters Road, Nag's Head, Holloway. After an argument over who should be served first, Mr McGrath left McDonald's with his purchases and Ciantar, who did not wait to collect the cheeseburger and fries he had ordered, followed him up the street and without any provocation or warning stabbed him in the back. Mr McGrath died at the scene. The crime was caught on CCTV. On sentencing him to life imprisonment Ciantar was told it would be at least fifteen years before he could be considered for parole. Judge Richard Hawkins said, 'You stabbed him without mercy with a large kitchen knife. He came to an end in that sudden and brutal way. I conclude you intended to kill.'

James Seaton, Finsbury Park, 2005

On 30 November 2005, the battered and almost decapitated body of thirty-nine-year-old Jacqueline Queen was found by a dog walker in a park in East Finchley. Her Scots lover, forty-six-year-old gravedigger and unemployed bricklayer James Seaton, of Gainsborough House, Thorpedale Road, Finsbury Park, admitted killing her but claimed he was suffering from mental illness. He battered her to death with a claw hammer and sawed through her neck with a knife after she had spurned him for a lesbian lover. Prosecutor Brian Altman said at Seaton's trial at Snaresbrook Crown Court in October 2006, 'He refused to believe it when Miss Queen said she was a lesbian. The defendant refused to believe that she no longer wanted him.' Seaton was found guilty of murder and sentenced to life imprisonment on Friday 13 October 2006. After the trial was over, investigating officer Detective Inspector John Nicholson said outside the court, 'I am pleased the jury recognised that James Seaton was neither provoked into his actions nor was suffering from such abnormality of the mind that he could claim the defence of diminished responsibility.'

Sources and Further Reading

The Stuart Age, Barry Coward, Longman, London, 1980.

Who's Who in Stuart Britain, C P Hill, Shepheard-Walwyn, London, 1988.

The Stuarts, B T Batsford, J P Kenyon, London, 1958.

The Strange Death of Edmund Godfrey, Alan Marshall, Sutton Publishing, Stroud, 1999.

Murder in London – A Topographical Guide to Famous Crimes, R Angus Downie, Arthur Barker, London 1973.

The History of Clerkenwell, William John Pinks, 2nd edition, 1880.

Criminal Islington, Keith Sugden (ed.), Islington Archeology & History Society, London, 1989.

The Common Hangman, James Bland, Ian Henry Publications, Hornchurch, 1984.

The Chronicles of Newgate, Arthur Griffiths, Chapman and Hall, London, 1883.

Notable British Trials: Franz Müller, Arthur Griffiths (ed.), William Hodge & Company, London, 1911.

Notable British Trials: The Trial of Hawley Harvey Crippen, Filson Young (ed.), William Hodge & Company, London, Edinburgh and Glasgow, 1920.

Notable British Trials: The Seddons, Filson Young, William Hodge & Company, London Edinburgh and Glasgow, 1914.

The Murders of the Black Museum 1870–1970, Gordon Honeycombe, Bloomsbury, London, 1982.

Crippen Case, Old Bailey Records CRIM1/117.

Crippen Case, Scotland Yard Files MEP03/198.

Crippen Case, Director of Public Prosecutions DPP1/13.

I Caught Crippen, Walter Dew, Blackie & Son, London & Glasgow, 1938.

The Crippen File, Jonathan Goodman, Allison & Busby, London, 1985.

Famous Crimes of Recent Times, Edgar Wallace, William Le Quex, Herbert Vivian, Sir Max Pemberton, Trevor Allen, Sir John Hall and Edgar Jepson, George Newnes Limited, London, n.d.

Ethel Le Neve: Her Life Story with the True Account of their Flight and her Friendship with Dr Crippen, first published in *Lloyd's Weekly* of 6 and 13 November 1910, and by John Long Ltd, London, 1910. (This edition published by the Daisy Bank Printing & Publishing Co., Gorton, Manchester, 1911.)

Lord High Executioner, Howard Engel, Firefly Books, Willowdale, Ontario, 1996.

Crimes That Thrilled The World, John Garland, Mellifont Press, London, 1937.

Prick Up Your Ears, John Lahr, Penguin, London, 1978.

The Orton Diaries, John Lahr (ed.), Methuen, London, 1986.

The Murder Guide, Brian Lane Robinson, London, 1991.

Murder Guide to London, Martin Fido Grafton, London, 1986.

The New Murderers Who's Who, JHH Gaute and Robin Audell Harrap, London, 1989.

North London Murders, Geoffrey Howse, Sutton, Stroud, Gloucestershire, 2005.

The A–Z of London Murders, Geoffrey Howse, Wharncliffe Books, 2007.

Lloyds Weekly News, 23 October 1910.

News of The World, 27 December 1914, 7 February 25 June 1915.

The Times, 11 July, 11, 15 November 1864, 25 October, 13, 14, 24 December 1890, 15 February, 20, 21, 22, May, 10, 11 June 1896, 13, 14, 15, 16, 18, 19 December 1899, 10 January 1900, 14, 16, 17, 18, 19 December 1907, 25, 26 January 1909, 25, 29 July, 2 August, 19, 20, 21, 22, 24, 26 October, 23 November 1910, 5, 6, 8, 9, 1, 12, 13, 14, 15 March 1912, 5, 9 January 1926, 4, 5, 9, 11, 18 January 1933, 16 February 1948, 30, 31 July, 27, 29 October, 14, 16 December 1954, 14 July 1955, 6, 9 May 1959, 10 August 1967, 14 December 1974.

Daily Telegraph, 5 September 1864, 10, 19 August 1967.

Daily Mail, 16, 18, 19, 25, 26, 27, 28, 29, 30, 1, 2, 3, 6 August 1910, 10 August 1967.

Daily Mirror, 30 January 1909, 24, March, 2 July 1915, 13, 14, July 1955.

Islington Daily Gazette and North London Tribune, 2, 19 January 1903.

Islington Gazette, 14 May 1963.

Evening News, London, 14, 15, 17, 19, 20, 21, 22, 24 February, 7, 26 March, 7, 9, 13, 14, 16, 23, 29, 30 April, 1, 4, 6, 7, 16, 19, 20, 21, 22, 29 May, 5, 9 June 1896, 18, 19, 20, 21, 22, 25 October, 23 November 1910, 4, 5, 6, 7, 8, 9, 12, 15 March, 18 April 1912, 15, 16, 17, 18, 19 December 1958, 8 May 1959, 14 December 1974.

Evening Standard, London, 14, 15, 17 February, 13, 14, 17 April, 19, 20, 21 May, 9 June 1896, 4, 5, 6, 7, 8, 9, 11, 12, 13, 14 March, 18 April 1912, 26 January 1950, 15, 18 December 1958, 1, 6, 8 May 1959, 4 September 1967.

North London Press, 18 May 1962.

Illustrated Police News, January 5 1867, January 12 1933, May 27 1937.

The Penny Illustrated Paper and Illustrated Times, 18 April 1896.

Morning Advertiser, 15 July 1910.

Index